My Gift to You

Welcome!

I am so glad that you picked up my book and are taking the time to invest in yourself. Your future self and your team will thank you for it!

To help you get the most out of this book, I have created a free workbook that you can access and download from my website. It's the perfect companion to the book and will help you capture your responses to the questions and exercises presented at the end of each day's reading. Find it at www. eliseboggs.com/eqworkbook.

Praise for *Lead Anyone*

"If you're ready to take your leadership to the next level, *Lead Anyone* by Elise Boggs Morales is the road map you've been searching for. Drawing on years of experience in both the military and the marketplace, I can confidently say this book is a game changer for anyone eager to master the art of leadership.

In just 28 days, Elise guides you through a simple yet powerful journey to develop key leadership skills. Each day offers a bite-sized lesson that blends practical wisdom with real-world examples, giving you immediate tools to apply emotional intelligence in your leadership approach.

What makes *Lead Anyone* truly stand out is its practical, no-nonsense advice. Elise encourages deep self-reflection, helping you assess your self-awareness and develop the discipline needed for effective self-management. But she doesn't stop there—Elise also delves into the often-overlooked areas of social awareness and relationship management, providing actionable strategies that will enhance both your professional and personal connections.

The principles in *Lead Anyone* are more than just leadership tactics—they are the foundation for building lasting, meaningful relationships. Whether you're leading a team, managing clients, or simply striving to be a more influential individual, this book equips you with the tools to succeed.

If you're ready to push past your limits and unlock your true leadership potential, I wholeheartedly recommend reading *Lead Anyone*. It's time to invest in yourself and elevate your leadership to new heights!"

— Mark Leposky, executive vice president and chief supply chain officer at Topgolf Callaway Brands Corp. and board member of Flux Power Holdings

"*Lead Anyone* by Elise Boggs Morales offers a nuanced exploration of leadership, focusing on integrating emotional intelligence principles to enhance team dynamics, innovation, and organizational performance. The book provides a structured approach that enables leaders to cultivate skills such as empathy, effective communication, and conflict management, thereby procuring an environment of trust and collaboration. Through detailed case studies and actionable insights, Elise demonstrates how adaptive leadership strategies drive meaningful change and elevate individual and team performance. A must-read for all leaders."

— Robert B. Ekoniak, Navy SEAL (retired)

"In a time in which emotional intelligence distinguishes great leaders, Elise demystifies leadership development with straightforward daily exercises. Both seasoned and emerging leaders will enhance their skills by focusing on either strengthening current abilities or addressing weaknesses. The skills Elise teaches are essential for anyone aspiring to lead, paving the way for a new generation of impactful leaders."

— Jenna Knudsen, managing principal at CO Architects

"I have been in the civil engineering consulting business, a highly technical field, for 27 years. My career began with a focus on engineering itself before progressing into project management and leadership roles. Along the way, I've read countless leadership books and articles in an effort to develop the skills they don't teach in school. I only wish *Lead Anyone* had been available 15 years ago!

This book does a fantastic job of distilling the core principles of leadership into one accessible resource. It presents them in a way that is easy to understand and immediately applicable to daily routines. The 28-day structure—focusing on one leadership topic per day—makes learning both manageable and engaging. I especially appreciated the format: each skill is introduced with background, reinforced with a real-world story, and followed by a practical exercise. This approach made working through the book a real joy—I actually looked forward to it each day!

Best of all, *Lead Anyone* isn't just a one-time read. Each concept is easy to revisit whenever needed, making this a resource I'll keep close at hand for years to come. Whether you're new to leadership or a seasoned veteran, this book is a must-read. Highly recommended!"

— Scott Kuebler, CEO at KPFF Consulting Engineers

"Great leadership starts with leading ourselves and thrives on continuous improvement. *Lead Anyone* not only tells you what to do but also shows you how to become the best leader you can be. Whether you're a CEO or at any other level within an organization, this book offers valuable insights and actionable guidance for leadership growth."

"I have spent a decade working side by side with Elise in leadership development for my company and have witnessed firsthand the transformation that leaders are capable of with her coaching and this tool set. My own development from applying these tools under Elise's guidance has been a game changer. What a gift to have this content packaged into convenient lessons that are easy to apply and practice. This book can and will change your trajectory."

"In Elise's must-read new book, *Lead Anyone,* she introduces leaders to her groundbreaking leadership philosophy starting with emotional intelligence. Her hard-won wisdom born from decades of experience leads the reader to action items that will change leadership styles forever. *Lead Anyone* sets the stage for anyone who is ready to make positive change by instituting small measurable steps following her easy-to-apply method."

Lead Anyone

28 DAYS TO TRANSFORM YOUR TEAM
THROUGH THE POWER OF EMOTIONAL
INTELLIGENCE

ELISE BOGGS MORALES

LEAD ANYONE

28 DAYS TO TRANSFORM YOUR TEAM THROUGH THE POWER OF EMOTIONAL INTELLIGENCE

ELISE BOGGS MORALES

To all the leaders I have worked alongside and whose many stories have shaped this book.

CONTENTS

Published 2025

ISBN 979-8-9918427-0-9 (paperback)

ISBN 979-8-9918427-1-6 (eBook)

For information about special discounts available for bulk purchases, contact the author: https://www.eliseboggs.com/contact.

The ability to deal with people is as purchasable a commodity as sugar or coffee. And I will pay more for that ability than for any other under the sun.

— JOHN D. ROCKEFELLER

Introduction

Leadership expert and author John C. Maxwell says that "Everything rises and falls on leadership."[1] In my experience working with thousands of leaders across many industries over the last seventeen years, I couldn't agree more. Because of our profound influence, leaders are at the heart of every organization's success or failure. The challenge is that most of us were never taught to be leaders.

Before we were leaders, we were individual contributors who stood out because of our smarts, technical competencies, and ability to get results. Then we became leaders, and suddenly we were not just responsible for our own performance but also the performance of others. Leadership requires the abilities to leverage the strengths of our teams, engage different personalities, get alignment for goals, and navigate interpersonal challenges, all of which can be very emotionally draining. Leadership is a completely unique skill

---

1. John C. Maxwell, *The 21 Irrefutable Laws of Leadership: Follow Them and People Will Follow You* (Thomas Nelson, Inc., 1998).

set that requires as much training and experience as the technical parts of our jobs, yet in spite of this, leadership is not taught alongside our technical education. As a result, people who are used to being very successful in their work may be caught off guard when they get promoted into leadership, and they may feel frustrated and unsuccessful. Many leaders think they are alone in this struggle, but it's a very common challenge.

Whether you are leading an organization or you are a leader within an organization, what would you say is your organization's current investment in ongoing leadership development? A recent Forbes Coaches Council article notes that in 2020, "organizations worldwide spent approximately $357 billion on corporate training," but only 25 percent of that went to leadership development programs.[2] This is another factor that might help explain why many leaders are struggling—there isn't enough investment being directed toward their ongoing development. In my experience, organizations often do one-and-done training, meaning leadership development is treated like a task to be checked off a list. Usually one to two trainings are scheduled per year, and this does provide some general exposure, but it isn't enough to allow leaders to experience any real impact. Leadership is an art that must be cultivated over time through feedback, training, practice, and continuous reinforcement. Limiting leadership development to annual leadership training is like taking one cooking class and expecting to cook at a chef's level.

What is the impact of not investing in our own leadership and creating opportunities within our organizations for other leaders? One of the biggest areas of impact is turnover and

2. Afsheen Ismail-Way, "Achieving Higher Returns on Your Leadership Development Spend," Forbes Coaches Council, July 19, 2023, https://www.forbes.com/councils/forbescoachescouncil/2023/07/19/achieving-higher-returns-on-your-leadership-development-spend/.

retention. You may have heard the saying "People join organizations but leave bosses." One survey found that 57 percent of people have quit their jobs because of their managers, and another 32 percent have considered leaving because of them.[3] I have worked firsthand with organizations that have been able to retain employees during extremely volatile economic times because of good leadership, even with competitors offering pay increases. Other areas affected by a lack of investment in leadership development include engagement, performance, profitability, and customer satisfaction. So why is there not more of an investment being made?

In my experience helping organizations design leadership development programs, I have observed that there's often the belief that if an employee is a high performer, they will inherently hold the skills to lead a team as well. But, as I have mentioned already, leadership is its own skill set, so the skills that got you promoted are not the same skills needed to successfully lead a team. Another reason for the lack of investment is confusion about what skills to focus on and how to cultivate them. Unlike tactical, measurable management skills, which tend to be more task-focused, leadership skills are a bit more nuanced and predominantly people-focused. This adds a complexity that may seem harder to quantify since the impact of focused leadership effort is often experienced over time. When I got my master's degree in organizational leadership and development back in 2005, at the time, the US had a plethora of management programs but only a handful of leadership programs.

In this book, I have distilled down the leadership skills that are going to make the greatest impact for you in the

3. "The Frontline Leader Project: Exploring the Most Critical Segment of Leaders," Development Dimensions International, 2019, https://media. ddiworld.com/research/frontline-leader-project_research_ebook_ddi.pdf.

shortest amount of time. They are the skills that will allow you to lead anyone, not just the select few who are most similar to you and easiest to lead. At its core, leadership is a relationship with followers. People don't follow a position; they follow a person they trust. Think of your own life; you are probably more willing to give commitments of your time, energy, and other resources to those you have relationships with than those you don't. It's the same for the people on your team. Because our success as leaders is ultimately measured by the results we achieve, cultivating relationships with our teams often lives on the back burner or falls out of the picture altogether. The art of leadership is learning how to get results *through* your team. The quality of your results will always reflect the quality of your relationships. So how do you cultivate these relationship-building skills? That is the focus of this book.

The skills associated with leading people have been called "soft skills," which deters many leaders from believing they are relevant to the bottom line. Some equate soft skills with weak leadership and believe they are not essential to profitability and organizational success, but that couldn't be further from the truth. When you build the skills I've laid out for you, the results of stronger engagement, performance, and retention (both employee and customer) will all have a direct impact on your bottom line.

Within the leadership skill set is a foundational set of four skills known as emotional intelligence. These skills are the specific and measurable relationship-building skills that set exceptional leaders apart. Anything with the word *emotion* in it can be off-putting to some, as it conjures up feelings of discomfort that things are getting too personal or makes them assume that they have to be "touchy-feely." Some fear that they aren't built to be good at those types of interactions. I understand, but I want to pose something to you.

When you look at what drains you most about leading your team, I am willing to bet it is the interpersonal dynamics. In order to address that, you have to zero in on the skills that specifically address that challenge.

That is the focus of emotional intelligence. And yes, it is uncomfortable at times, but it is purposeful discomfort. Are you uncomfortable navigating conflict with others? Having direct and productive performance conversations? Knowing what to say when a personal challenge is affecting someone's professional performance? If you are like most leaders I know, you can relate to these challenges. And while these challenges never go away, with emotional intelligence, you'll find yourself better able to navigate them. The discomfort of cultivating emotional intelligence skills pays off tenfold when you find that it allows you to more skillfully handle the leadership tasks and conversations you used to avoid.

At the end of the day, leaders want to get the job done with the least amount of resistance from their teams as possible. Leading with emotional intelligence is *the* skill set that will equip you to lead anyone. While these skills can seem undefined, I'm here to demystify them for you and give you practical actions you can take every day to cultivate and improve them. It's often the small things done over time that make the biggest difference. I invite you to come on the adventure of transforming your team over the next twenty-eight days through the power of emotional intelligence!

WHAT *IS* EMOTIONAL INTELLIGENCE, ANYWAY?

Before we go any further, let's define exactly what we're talking about. While there are a lot of wordy definitions out there, I'll explain emotional intelligence in simple layman's terms. *Emotional intelligence is the ability to identify and manage your emotions, to accurately read others' emotions, and to adjust your approach to effectively manage your relationships.* Emotions are important things to manage because they guide behaviors. How we behave influences how others perceive us (both positively and negatively) and can either support or undermine our ability to influence desired outcomes in both our professional and personal lives.

So why haven't you heard of emotional intelligence before —or, if you have, why isn't it talked about more? The term has been around since the '60s, but it didn't get *really* popular until 1995 with the release of Daniel Goleman's best-selling book *Emotional Intelligence: Why It Can Matter More than IQ.* In 1998, Goleman published a follow-up article for the *Harvard Business Review* entitled "What Makes a Leader?"[4] Both make a case for a specific set of skills and characteristics that drive leadership performance. The *Harvard Business Review* article caught the attention of Johnson & Johnson, spurring them to conduct a study that confirmed the strong link between high-performing leaders and emotional competencies.[5] Emotional intelligence has now become a more familiar term, challenging the way leaders view their roles. Effective leadership used to be defined by a more command-and-control style that created a sense of compliance at best. Nowadays, leaders are expected to be able to inspire true commitment from their followers, and this requires a completely different set of skills. The good news is that these skills are not all innate talents but learned capabilities that can be worked on and developed.

Recently, I was on a plane seated next to the CEO of a large company. When I asked him what he thought was one

4. Daniel Goleman, "What Makes a Leader," *Harvard Business Review*, 1998.
5. Kathleen Cavallo and Dottie Brienza, "Emotional Competence and Leadership Excellence at Johnson & Johnson: The Emotional Intelligence and Leadership Study," Consortium for Research on Emotional Intelligence in Organizations, 2002, http://www.eiconsortium.org/reports/jj_ei_study.html.

of the greatest factors in his success, he said that learning emotional intelligence had changed his life. He shared that learning to master his emotions and build relationships with people across all levels of the organization had allowed him to get work done easier and faster. He also saw the difference it made in keeping his top talent and creating a better culture. He had no idea I was writing a book on the topic. Our conversation provided more evidence of the transformative power of these skills for those who are willing to learn them.

So how do you learn the skills that really matter in a sea of information about leadership? You don't have to read twenty leadership books, attend a bunch of conferences, and get a leadership degree to become a great leader. Much of that is theory anyway, and what leaders really need is someone to take the complexity of leadership and simplify it into daily actions that are practical and get results quickly. Consider the book you hold in your hand a cheat sheet for doing just that! What you need to know is how to apply the skills most effective for leadership, so that's what we're going to focus on.

The book contains twenty-eight daily readings that will each take you about five to seven minutes to read. Each day, you will explore a skill that is essential for leading yourself and your team well. At times, we will hit a skill twice from different perspectives based on the ones people tend to struggle with the most and have questions around. To illustrate how transformative these skills can be, I'll share real stories of leaders who were having challenges in leading their teams and how they were coached to success by strengthening their abilities in emotional intelligence. You won't just get theoretical ideas but will witness each skill in action. Then, I will give you one or more simple and practical actions you can take to practice the skill and set yourself on the path to getting the same results. By learning and applying one new emotional intelligence skill per day, you will be continuously making small changes that will have immediate and long-lasting impacts on your ability to lead anyone.

My expertise in leadership spans both theory and practice. As a student and professor of leadership, I've delved deep into its academic foundations. As a practitioner, I've worked hands-on with thousands of leaders across a large cross section of industries, applying these same principles in real-world scenarios. I'm certified in emotional intelligence and have trained and coached leaders in these skills since 2008. I've led high-performing teams in the nonprofit and for-profit sectors, both domestically and internationally.

If there's one thing I've learned from my time working with leaders across nearly every context, at the end of the day, leaders want to get the job done with as little resistance from their teams as possible. Leading with emotional intelligence is the skill set that will get you there. These skills are within your reach; I'm here to demystify them for you and to give you practical actions you can take every day to improve them. It's often the small things done over time that make the biggest difference. I invite you to come on the adventure of creating your dream team!

WHAT TO EXPECT

A great place to start to understand emotional intelligence is learning the four main competencies that build on each other. These are the following:

1. Self-awareness
2. Self-management
3. Social awareness
4. Relationship management

This book is divided into four parts based on these competencies. Each part digs deeper into specific skills and actions you can take to develop that competency.

Self-awareness and self-management have to do with leading yourself. You cannot lead others well until you have learned to lead yourself well. Social awareness and relationship management, on the other hand, have to do with your ability to make meaningful connections with others and have influence in those relationships.

HOW TO GET THE MOST OUT OF THIS BOOK

I recommend reading first thing in the morning and focusing on one day's reading at a time. Next, plan to do the suggested action within twenty-four hours. If that's not possible, continue on to the next day's reading but plan to take the action as soon as you are able. Of course, none of the actions are mandated, but you are guaranteed to accelerate your progress in these skill sets when you intentionally put them into practice. Each day's reading is designed to be quick and powerful.

Now that you have the lay of the land, let's get started!

To know your baseline as we dive in, you may want to consider taking an emotional intelligence assessment to gain some insight into your current competency in emotional intelligence. Free assessments are available online, but if you want more in-depth results, you can find an assessment (the same one I use with my clients) available for purchase on my website at www.eliseboggs.com/courses.

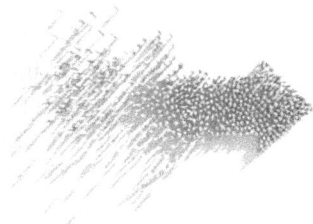

Part I

Self-Awareness

The first core competency of leading anyone is **self-awareness**.

The more self-aware you are, the more likely you are to understand the things you are doing that are either helping or hindering your ability to effectively lead your team. People high in self-awareness are able to recognize their emotions and how they affect their actions. They can also identify their strengths and weaknesses and name their conflict triggers, and they are in touch with the things they are passionate about and those that light them up. They have clearly defined values and recognize the influence their words and behaviors have on others.

In a series of surveys, organizational psychologist Tasha Eurich found that "although 95% of people think they're self-aware, only 10 to 15% actually are."[1] This highlights a

---

1. Tasha Eurich, "Working with People Who Aren't Self-Aware," Harvard Business Review, October 19, 2018, https://hbr.org/2018/10/working-with-people-who-arent-self-aware.

common theme I have seen with struggling leaders: the gap between how we see ourselves and how others see us. The best ways to close the gap are practicing self-reflection, taking assessments that increase our self-knowledge, and seeking out feedback from others, but unfortunately, good feedback is often hard to come by, especially as we go further up the leadership ladder!

This first part of the book will cover three core skills to help you increase your self-awareness:

1. Emotional self-awareness
2. Accurate self-assessment
3. Personal power

While your team may need to grow in certain areas, the leader must grow first! You are the person with the greatest influence on your team. When you take the initiative to get an accurate view of yourself, you now have the insight needed to shift to a more effective approach. When you shift how you are showing up as a leader, there will be a positive ripple effect in how your team responds to you. Leading yourself first puts you back in the driver's seat, which is where the ability to transform your team begins, so let's get started!

Day 1
Know Your Hot Buttons

There are three things [extremely] hard: steel, a diamond, and to know one's self.

— BENJAMIN FRANKLIN

W e all have hot buttons, whether we want to admit it or not. Hot buttons are those things that trigger an emotional response because something you value is being threatened. If you value deadlines being met, a hot button could be delays or excuses. If you value being on time, a team member arriving to a meeting late could put you in a bad mood. Whether you are the type of leader who wears your emotions on your sleeve or are more reserved, being aware of your hot buttons helps you to manage them. If your hot buttons are left unmanaged, your team will learn to walk on eggshells around you or may find you very difficult to read. This will prevent your team from having the safe and trusting relationship with you that they need to do their best work.

3

Today, we are focusing on increasing our levels of **emotional self-awareness**.

WHAT IS EMOTIONAL SELF-AWARENESS?

Emotional self-awareness is the ability to recognize and understand our emotions and how they influence our behavior. In the context of emotional intelligence at work, cultivating emotional self-awareness means learning our hot buttons so that we can become more mindful of our automatic reactions and respond in ways that support good relationships with our teams.

BENEFITS OF EMOTIONAL SELF-AWARENESS

This skill is foundational for learning to manage our emotions. Leaders with this skill listen to their body signals and can name their feelings and why they feel them. Instead of automatically reacting to situations that trigger their hot buttons, they are mindful and intentional in how they respond. They recognize that their moods greatly affect their team morale. Research by Korn Ferry Hay Group found that 92 percent of leaders skilled in emotional self-awareness had high-energy and high-performance teams.[1]

SYMPTOMS THAT YOU MAY NEED TO BUILD YOUR SKILL SET IN EMOTIONAL SELF-AWARENESS

- You tend to get easily irritated and frustrated,

---

1. Daniel Goleman, "What Is Emotional Self Awareness?," Korn Ferry, accessed September 19, 2024, https://www.kornferry.com/insights/this-week-in-leadership/what-is-emotional-self-awareness-2019.

causing you to say and do things that have a
negative impact on your team.

- You feel stressed most of the time, causing other
areas of your life to suffer.
- You have a difficult time identifying what you are
feeling and why.

SUSAN, EXECUTIVE, NONPROFIT

Susan was at risk of losing her entire executive team. Fortunately, she was able to turn things around before it was too late and she lost her best talent.

When I met Susan, I was immediately impressed by her go-getter spirit. She had an amazing capacity to get things done, and she was passionate about her work. Her challenge was that she was unaware that the expression of her unbridled emotions was having a significant impact on her team. When one of her hot buttons was triggered, she quickly became angry, saying things and behaving in ways that began to erode her team's sense of safety and trust. When confronted, she became defensive and blamed the team's performance and shortcomings for her response. Because reacting this way was such a well-formed habit, she was completely unaware of how she was feeling and reacting in the moment.

Susan reached out for coaching after several key people on her executive team threatened to leave. After speaking with each person on her team, I was able to identify themes of common hot-button moments. I presented these to Susan and asked her to identify what she was feeling in her body in those moments (such as heat moving through her body, quickened heartbeat, or tense muscles), what emotions she was feeling at those times (for example, frustration, anger, or disappointment), and why she was feeling those feelings

5

(maybe her expectations were not being met, she was feeling alone as a leader, or she believed there was a lack of initiative being taken).

It is very difficult to manage our behaviors until we can increase our awareness of the emotions behind them. Going through the methodical process described above provided a framework for Susan to see her hot-button situations with greater clarity. This provided the data Susan needed to manage her emotions proactively rather than being at the mercy of her in-the-moment reactions. (We will discuss managing emotions in detail on day 4.)

Once Susan understood what she was feeling and why, she also became more attuned to her body's signals when her hot buttons were being pressed. This increase in emotional awareness was the foundation for all the work to follow. Susan remained committed to the process, and within just a couple of months, she was showing up completely differently with her team. She began to realize that her leadership was the cause of her frustrations and performance issues with her team, not the other way around. In a relatively short amount of time, Susan was able to rebuild a sense of trust and safety with her team. Nearly a year later, everyone on her executive team has stayed, and the team is more aligned and productive than ever!

Some of you will relate to Susan's story; when your hot buttons get pressed, you express your emotions. Others may internalize your emotions when your hot buttons get pressed. You may avoid expressing your emotions or addressing situations. Whichever group you fall into, increasing your emotional self-awareness is key.

ACTION STEP

Want to get results like Susan's? Here's what you can do.

Identify Your Hot Buttons

Write down your hot buttons or ask your team if they can recall any hot-button moments you've had. If you are unsure, recall instances when the things you value felt threatened and this caused an emotional reaction inside of you.

Now write down what you were feeling in your body, what emotion you were experiencing, and why you were feeling that way. If you need help identifying the emotion, you can do a Google Images search for emotions and choose from a list (or use this list: https://www.pinterest.com/pin/621848661017537988/). You can also refer to Susan's example above for ideas.

Reflect: How does capturing your hot buttons in this way create clarity? How does this data give you insights into how to manage your emotions more productively?

Day 2

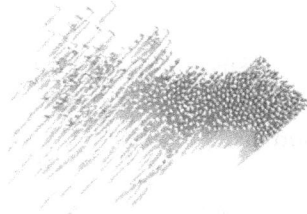

Minding the Gap

Knowing yourself is the beginning of all wisdom.

— ATTRIBUTED TO ARISTOTLE

If you have ever ridden the London Underground, you have probably heard the words "Mind the gap" over the loudspeaker when the train doors open. The announcement is an essential reminder to bring us back from any distractions so that we focus and become aware of the space between the platform and the train and can cross safely. If we fail to pay attention, we might injure ourselves and others. Similarly, a gap can exist between the way we see ourselves as leaders and the way we are seen by others. If we do not "Mind the gap," we may unknowingly and unintentionally communicate and behave in ways that undermine our effectiveness as leaders.

Today, we are focusing on increasing our levels of **accurate self-assessment**.

WHAT IS ACCURATE SELF-ASSESSMENT?

This self-awareness skill is foundational to building healthy self-image and relationships. Accurate self-assessment means having an accurate view of yourself—including both your strengths and weaknesses—that doesn't differ greatly from how others perceive you. Cultivating a sense of accurate self-assessment is a lifelong journey, but in the context of emotional intelligence at work, it means proactively seeking feedback and making adjustments to build stronger relationships with others.

BENEFITS OF ACCURATE SELF-ASSESSMENT

Leaders strong in this skill lead with confidence, having an accurate view of their strengths and capabilities. They acknowledge their blind spots and are committed to growth and improvement. They aren't afraid to ask for help and create transparent and authentic cultures. In my experience, the higher leaders rise within their organizations, the less likely they are to receive honest and constructive feedback, which is the very thing they need to close the perception gap.

SYMPTOMS THAT YOU MAY NEED TO BUILD YOUR SKILL SET IN ACCURATE SELF-ASSESSMENT

- You don't regularly ask for feedback from your team.
- You set unrealistic goals for yourself and your team.
- It feels like you are often misunderstood or often unintentionally offend your team.

ROBERT, EXECUTIVE, TECH COMPANY

One of the most powerful stories of leadership transformation I have experienced was with my client, Robert. In six months, Robert went from being on the chopping block at his company to being one of his company's most beloved leaders. When I first met Robert, I was impressed by his intelligence and experience—he had spent over thirty years in his industry. He was a master of his craft and was well respected for his technical competencies. I was brought in to be his coach because of the constant stream of HR complaints about him. When presented with some of the complaints, Robert was frustrated and defensive. He just wanted to get the job done without having to deal with the interpersonal drama of his team. It was also clear that he didn't enjoy leading and preferred to work on his own without having to depend on others. He viewed his team as a hindrance rather than an asset. I have found this to be a very common viewpoint of frustrated leaders. Many feel that if only their teams were "easier," they could lead effectively. Can you relate?

I suggested that Robert participate in a Leadership 360. This is an assessment where the leader receives feedback about their leadership effectiveness from all levels of their organization. When Robert's Leadership 360 feedback came back and he saw how his team and colleagues perceived him, Robert felt depressed and discouraged.

My job as a coach is to remind leaders that feedback provides the data needed to change things. Until we have data, we are shooting in the dark. While the data can be difficult to digest at first, those leaders courageous enough to move past the discomfort find that the data gives them what they need to transform themselves and their teams in amazing ways!

Robert and I chose to focus on three pieces of feedback at a time and identify specific actions to address them. Robert's team conveyed that he was inaccessible, not mentally present in meetings, and neglecting to use interoffice communication channels. To address these three pieces of feedback, Robert spent one month focusing on communicating when he was out of the office and how he could be reached. He also designated specific office hours when his team could ask him questions about projects. Finally, he prioritized providing more timely feedback and answers to questions, bringing value to meetings and finding ways to serve the younger team members with his experience, and using the instant communication channels for the projects he was overseeing.

These seemingly small tweaks made a *huge* difference! In just one month's time, Robert was able to reestablish a strong connection with his team. As a result, his team became more engaged and began completing projects more quickly and efficiently. Robert also found himself more excited about engaging with his team. He developed a love for mentoring and passing along his industry knowledge to the next generation. He went from wanting to work alone to fully leveraging his team's assets to do remarkable work.

Robert and I continued to focus on just three pieces of feedback at a time. By the six-month mark, Robert had become one of the most beloved leaders, especially among younger employees, in his company. Years later, he has continued to maintain this connection with his team, which enables him to do great work.

ACTION STEP

Want to get results like Robert's? Here's what you can do.
(Choose one or both of the following options.)

Informal Mini 360

Complete an informal Mini 360. Write down your top five leadership strengths and the top five areas in which your leadership needs development. Then choose five people who work with you closely (ideally people from various levels of your organization) to answer the same questions. Compare the answers you wrote down to those you receive from others. Create a list of actions to address the most prominent themes you notice from the feedback.

Formal Leadership 360

Participate in a formal Leadership 360 assessment. Some of the benefits of doing an official 360 include the following:

1. Feedback from an unlimited number of raters (both inside and outside of your company)
2. A completely anonymous and confidential process
3. A trained consultant to facilitate the process and help you interpret your results

If you are interested in learning more, go to my website to learn about the benefits of 360s and how they can help you and your team achieve your leadership goals: https://www.eliseboggs.com/leadership-360s.

Day 3
You've Got the Power

Leadership is the capacity and will to rally men and women to a common purpose and the character which inspires confidence.

— BERNARD MONTGOMERY

What do Mother Teresa, Martin Luther King Jr., Malala Yousafzai, and Winston Churchill have in common? Each of these diverse leaders had a vision of the world they wanted to create. Each took a stand in times of extreme adversity and achieved great things.

I had the opportunity to visit Calcutta and volunteer at Mother Teresa's Home for the Dying in my twenties. One thing that struck me was how a woman so small in stature who had no personal wealth could gain worldwide influence and mobilize the resources to accomplish so much in her lifetime! It was Mother Teresa's clear vision for what she wanted to achieve that allowed her to make such a difference. This proved to me that a leader's sense of personal power is not limited to a particular prototype; it's a skill that any leader can cultivate.

Today, we are focusing on increasing our levels of **personal power**.

WHAT IS PERSONAL POWER?

Personal power is having a clear purpose and defined direction. Those with personal power have a strong inner locus of control instead of letting external factors set the direction of their lives. In the context of emotional intelligence at work, when we cultivate personal power, that gives us a strong sense of self and helps us feel empowered to go after the things we want.

BENEFITS OF PERSONAL POWER

This self-awareness skill is essential for building a sense of self-confidence and having influence in our relationships with others. Leaders strong in this skill know how to garner the confidence of those they lead. They have a clear vision and strong values, and they stand by their convictions when challenged. They are not afraid to have difficult conversations to protect the long-term health of their teams.

Your team can only hold as much confidence in you as you do in yourself. A leader with vague convictions, unclear vision, and a lack of follow-through will find themself frustrated with their team's results; in reality, their team will mirror their lack of clarity back to them. In contrast, the clearer a leader gets on their purpose, vision, direction, and values, the easier that leader is to follow.

SYMPTOMS THAT YOU MAY NEED TO BUILD YOUR SKILL SET IN PERSONAL POWER

- You find yourself being indecisive or overthinking leadership decisions.
- You notice that you are avoiding confrontations with your team, even if that is what is needed to solve a problem.
- You sometimes find it difficult to defend your ideas to your peers or team and can get easily swayed by others' opinions.

ADAM, CEO, ARCHITECTURAL FIRM

My client Adam is one of the best examples I know of the transformational effects of developing a strong sense of personal power. When I first met Adam, he had just taken over as CEO of a prominent architectural firm. His predecessor had held the position for over 20 years, so he was stepping into some big shoes. The previous leader's personality, leadership style, and priorities were very different from Adam's. He had led successfully, but things in the industry had changed, and Adam knew that for the company to continue to succeed, things could not operate as they always had.

One of the challenges that Adam faced was inheriting an executive team that had been with the company for twenty-five to thirty years. Most of the members of the team were at least ten years his senior.

The company's culture had a strong value of autonomy, which provided an appealing level of freedom, but this caused members to operate siloed from one another, and cultivating relationships was not prioritized. This prevented a sense of alignment from being created. The focus was on the work and on the client, not as much on strengthening the internal culture that supported the work. The company had experienced success, so why change? A compelling reason was the needs and desires of the new millennial workforce. They wanted a culture of purpose beyond the work, a strong sense of community with those they worked with, mentorship and career-development opportunities, and training in leadership and people skills.

Adam knew that changing the existing culture would be no easy task and would take time. It would also take a strong sense of personal power. He needed to establish his own leadership identity, including a clear vision for the firm and a compelling way of engaging and aligning his new team. He enlisted my help as his coach to create a strategic process for doing this. The first thing I suggested was that Adam create a leadership philosophy. This exercise allows a leader to get crystal clear about their values, determine what kind of leader they want to be, and identify their vision for the future. The philosophy serves as a guide for both decision-making and establishing priorities. It also informs some difficult conversations that may need to be had.

After Adam was able to get this clarity, we got to work. The first priority was to build rapport and relationships with the executive team. This established a sense of trust, resulting in greater levels of alignment and collaboration in leading the office. We did a series of engagement interviews top to bottom to gather valuable information about the company's strengths and areas where development was necessary. That data provided a road map for initiatives to invest in a more people-driven culture. Relationships are like glue. If people have a strong relationship with their leader and teammates, they are more likely to stay. A new position was created to oversee people operations. Leadership development and team trainings focused on people skills became the operative norm.

Now, ten years later, the firm has established a new culture to meet the new demands of both the industry and workforce. The firm is thriving, and Adam, although he was initially met with lots of resistance, has become a trusted and beloved leader. In fact, other firms are now taking note and emulating programs similar to Adam's in the hopes of achieving the same success.

That's the power of personal power!

ACTION STEP

Want to get results like Adam's? Here's what you can do.

Create Your Own Personal Leadership Philosophy

Write a personal leadership philosophy. This can be one to two paragraphs in length, and the inclusions do not have to be things that you practice perfectly, but the philosophy should include your aspirations. If you need inspiration, answer these questions first for guidance:

1. What are the qualities of the leaders you respect and admire the most?
2. What are your own leadership values?
3. How do you want others to describe you as a person and leader?
4. What is your personal cause?
5. What do you want to be able to influence through your leadership?

Once you have answered the questions, you can integrate your answers into your personal leadership philosophy. There are many examples online, but here are some specific examples that may inspire you in creating your own!

I lead with integrity by living by the values that I profess. I build a strong team where people are heard, feedback is welcomed, and the strengths and experiences of each person are fully leveraged. I intentionally pursue my own growth as a leader and create a culture of continual improvement.

I lead a team that achieves remarkable results. I inspire others with a clear and compelling vision and empower people to use their strengths and pursue their passions. I make myself accessible to mentor and guide my team, and I am intentional about creating a benchmark for leadership. I set lofty goals and create a sense of excitement to achieve big things.

Part II

Self-Management

Once you become self-aware, you have the insight needed to manage both your emotions and behaviors to get the outcomes you desire in your interactions with others. People high in self-management are intentional and action oriented. They also have good impulse control, can remain calm in trying situations, and are responsive rather than reactive when they are triggered. Self-management not only earns you the respect and trust of your team, but it also creates a safe environment where people can be productive and creative.

I mentioned earlier that people join organizations but leave bosses. Some of the most common reasons are related to a lack of self-management skills. If a leader cannot manage themself first, they are also going to struggle in leading their team. Leadership flows from the inside out.

In this section, we will cover seven core skills to help you increase your self-management:

1. Behavioral self-control
2. Integrity

3. Intentionality
4. Initiative and bias for action
5. Resilience
6. Stress management
7. Creativity and innovation

While a lack of self-management can create *compliance* in your team, mastering your emotions and behaviors can create a *genuine commitment* from your team. Organizations nationwide are spending billions in turnover costs every year when they don't have to be. Let's change that!

Day 4

Mastering Your Emotions

Better a patient person than a warrior, one with self-control than one who takes a city.

— PROVERBS 16:32 (NIV)

We've already discussed the familiar adage that "People join organizations but leave bosses." While research suggests that people leave companies for a number of reasons, I've experienced two significant factors linked to the relationship employees have with their bosses are worth noting: lack of interest in their career progression and incivility. I left my first two jobs after college because of incivility, despite loving the work I was doing. Incivility can take many forms, but I am going to narrow our focus to leaders who express their emotions in ways that undermine the relationships they have with their teams.

Today, we are focusing on increasing our levels of **behavioral self-control**.

WHAT IS BEHAVIORAL SELF-CONTROL?

Like other skills in self-management, this one starts with a strong foundation in emotional self-awareness (see day 1). When we are aware of what we are feeling and why, we have the information needed to manage that emotion. In the context of emotional intelligence at work, cultivating behavioral self-control means keeping disruptive emotions and impulses in check—mastering our emotions instead of letting them master us!

BENEFITS OF BEHAVIORAL SELF-CONTROL

Behavioral self-control helps you think clearly and stay focused under pressure. It's one of those core leadership skills that can make or break your ability to create the kinds of relationships you desire at every level. Leaders strong in this skill have strong impulse control, staying composed and positive even in trying moments. Incivility is expensive! According to a *Harvard Business Review* poll of 800 managers and employees in seventeen industries, here is the effect among employees:

- "48% intentionally decreased their work effort."
- "47% intentionally decreased the time spent at work."
- "38% intentionally decreased the quality of their work."
- "80% lost work time worrying about the incident."
- "63% lost work time avoiding the offender."
- "66% said that their performance declined."
- "78% said that their commitment to the organization declined."

- "12% said that they left their job because of the uncivil treatment."[1]

If leaders lacking behavioral self-control has been normalized in your industry, it can be a hard pattern to break, but it's well worth the effort for the rewards of engagement, performance, and retention from your team.

SYMPTOMS THAT YOU MAY NEED TO BUILD YOUR SKILL SET IN BEHAVIORAL SELF-CONTROL

- You find yourself getting immediately defensive when your team questions or challenges you.
- When something or someone triggers you, you tend to react first and think later.
- You find it challenging to maintain your composure and focus as a leader when stressed.

SUSAN, EXECUTIVE, NONPROFIT

Remember Susan from day 1? We'll continue her success story here.

Once Susan was more emotionally aware, we had the data to help her master her emotions rather than letting her emotions master her. In our initial exercise, Susan became aware that she felt a wave of heat in her body before she lost her cool. She had also discovered that her main hot button happens when she gives direction and her team asks a lot of questions. She feels angry when this happens.

In my experience, changing our behavior around our hot

---

1. Christine Porath and Christine Pearson, "The Price of Incivility," *Harvard Business Review*, January/February 2013, https://hbr.org/2013/01/the-price-of-incivility.

buttons rarely works. We have to go deeper to find out what's behind our unproductive reactions. Our reactions actually work in a sequence that looks like this:

Hot Button → Thought → Feeling → Reaction

Once we get triggered around our hot buttons, the immediate thought or story we tell ourselves about the situation leads to a feeling, and that feeling greatly influences our reaction. In Susan's case, the thought that immediately followed her team's questioning was "They don't trust or respect me." This thought led to feelings of anger, and she reacted with cutting and belittling remarks. Once we identified this, we now had a story to work with. If we could get clarity around the story, then perhaps new emotions and reactions could be cultivated and the hot button could lose its power.

The first question to ask around our stories is whether they are true. In Susan's case, the most efficient way to determine this was to ask her team what their intentions were in asking lots of questions after direction was given. I coached Susan to approach her team with curiosity rather than blame. Her team shared with her that they needed clarity, wanted to be in alignment, and wanted to ensure everything had been thought through. Ultimately, they wanted to get things right. Susan realized that the story she had been telling herself was inaccurate. Once she had an accurate story, the feeling that followed was understanding, and the reaction that now effortlessly followed was having a robust dialogue with her team.

She realized her team was helping her win by evaluating decisions from all angles.

We continued to address additional hot buttons. Sometimes the story Susan was telling herself about a situation was true. In that case, she had the opportunity to talk it through productively as a team and bring resolution.

Whether you are an external reactor like Susan or more of an internal stuffer, the method for mastering your emotions is the same. Susan now has tools for mastering her emotions when new hot buttons come up, and her team has stopped threatening to leave because a sense of trust and safety has been restored.

ACTION STEP

Want to get results like Susan's? Here's what you can do.

Change the Story Exercise

First, complete the action step in day 1 for emotional awareness.

Next, go through the following reaction sequence:

Hot Button → Thought → Feeling → Reaction

- What is a hot button you want to address?
- What is the thought or story you have about this trigger?
- What feeling do you have in response to that thought or story?
- What is your current reaction?

Now ask yourself...

- Am I certain this story is true? What can I do to get clarity?
- What is a new story that will lead to a different feeling?

- How does this information affect what I am now feeling?
- What will my response be going forward?

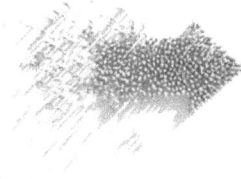

Day 5
Walk the Talk

The hypocrite's crime is that he bears false witness against himself.

— HANNAH ARENDT

My final assignment before earning my master's in leadership was to write a fifty-page paper on my leadership philosophy. When I thought back to the qualities exhibited by the leaders I respected the most, the quality of integrity was definitely at the top of my list. Later, when I became a professor, I asked each of my classes what they thought the most important qualities of a leader were. While there was not one universal answer, integrity was *always* in the top three.

I have found that it is not major breaches in integrity that most leaders struggle with, but rather the more subtle everyday compromises that undermine the trust others have in them. Integrity matters in the big things, but also in the seemingly small and insignificant things that add up.

Today, we are focusing on increasing our levels of **integrity**.

WHAT IS INTEGRITY?

Integrity is having strong moral and ethical values and consistently acting in alignment with those values. It's also the willingness to confront unethical actions in others. Leaders strong in this skill do the things author Brené Brown describes in her talk "The Anatomy of Trust," such as choosing courage over comfort, doing what's right versus what's fast, easy, or fun, and living their values, not just professing them.[1] In the context of emotional intelligence at work, cultivating integrity means making decisions based on our values instead of our emotions.

BENEFITS OF INTEGRITY

Like other self-management skills, integrity helps us build and maintain trust with other people. It inspires trust and confidence in your leadership. When people trust you, they follow you out of true commitment (rather than out of obligated compliance). Cultivating integrity within yourself also has the potential to create an overall company culture that values integrity and is accountable because integrity is modeled from the top.

1. Brené Brown, "SuperSoul Sessions: The Anatomy of Trust," Brene-Brown.com, November 1, 2015, video, 22:49, https://brenebrown.com/videos/anatomy-trust-video/.

SYMPTOMS THAT YOU MAY NEED TO BUILD YOUR SKILL SET IN INTEGRITY

- There is a gap between the values you profess and the values you practice.
- You tend to compromise your values when stressed or under pressure.
- You avoid confronting unethical behavior on your team.

MARK, MEDICAL DIRECTOR, HEALTH-CARE GROUP

I met Mark when his assistant introduced us during a business function. She shared that Mark had been experiencing high turnover on his team. As a result of the turnover, the company was quickly losing patients, and Mark's assistant wondered if I could help.

When I asked Mark what he thought the trouble might be, he shrugged and said that people just didn't have the kind of work ethic and commitment that they used to. He also talked about patients being high maintenance and said that certain physicians couldn't handle it. His assistant shot me a knowing look, the kind of look that told me that she knew the reasons for the turnover and they weren't the reasons Mark had identified.

I asked Mark if he wanted me to help him solve his turnover problem. While he was doubtful that we would discover anything he hadn't tried yet, he agreed.

The first thing we needed was feedback. Data is always the first thing you need to solve any problem. You can get the feedback you need through tools such as a Leadership 360 or through surveys or engagement interviews (see day 2). In situations like Mark's, when the number of interviews is twenty people or fewer and I want to ask a variety of questions about topics going beyond leadership, such as culture, organizational systems, and similar, I prefer to do engagement interviews. With Mark's team, I conducted a combination of individual and group interviews with his direct reports and key support staff. These engagement interviews provided an opportunity for follow-up questions, which surveys don't allow. I interviewed each of Mark's direct reports and a cross section of key support staff. For Mark, it was beneficial to have me on board to conduct the engagement interviews because having an outside consultant who protects confidentiality is key to getting honest feedback. Interviews can also be done by someone internal as long as (1) there are high levels of trust that confidentiality will be protected and (2) that internal person is skilled in converting data into clear themes that help inform necessary actions. (You can contact us at https://www.eliseboggs.com/contact to get guidance on what tool is the best fit for your situation, request support from our team, or both.)

I gathered the data, and the themes revealed a lack of integrity. People did not trust or respect Mark.

When I presented the info to Mark, he was taken aback. He considered himself a moral person and felt judged and misunderstood. I explained that people perceived him to have certain expectations of them that he didn't abide by himself. Those interviewed mentioned how he showed up late to meetings, didn't attend mandatory conferences and meetings, didn't listen without interrupting, and didn't follow through on deadlines and commitments.

Mark had what I call "leader amnesia," where leaders remember when others don't meet their standards but don't pay attention to their own adherence because they are the leaders. Somehow they think leadership means directing and holding others accountable to behavior they don't model themselves. Most of the time, this attitude isn't even conscious, but it's an unrecognized gap that costs leaders the retention of their best talent. No one wants to follow a leader who says "Do as I say, but not as I do."

Mark wondered if what he called "small" infractions could really be making that much of a difference with his team. I asked him to do an experiment for a month by addressing each of the infractions by shifting from just professing values to actually practicing those values. I also suggested he acknowledge the feedback he received from his team and give them permission to respectfully let him know if he was acting out of integrity. We didn't even need a month; the team dynamic changed drastically within just one week.

Mark continued to work on improving his integrity, and within several months, his turnover came to a screeching halt. Mark's sense of self-respect began to increase as well, as now he was living in alignment with his values and receiving the respect from his team that had previously eluded him.

ACTION STEP

Want to get results like Mark's? Here's what you can do.

Complete a Values Self-Audit

Create a table with three columns, "Professed Values," "Practiced Values," and "Examples." List a value in the first column, indicate whether you practice it in the second column with a yes or a no, and then list specific examples to support your answers in the third column.

This self-audit will require strong levels of self-awareness.

Bonus Action: Complete a Values Audit with Your Team

If you want to take your evaluation a step further, give the audit to your key team members and ask them to evaluate you as well. Simply create another copy of the chart and give it to your key team members, asking them to indicate whether they think you practice each of the values listed. Encourage them to provide specific examples. Compare your answers with the ones they provide.

Note: Once you have completed the audit process, come up with a list of actions you can take and commitments you can make to address any gaps between your professed and practiced behaviors.

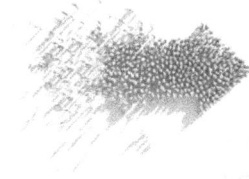

Day 6
Acting on Purpose

> Ultimately, human intentionality is the most powerful evolutionary force on this planet.

> — GEORGE LEONARD

One of the best decisions I made this year was hiring a business coach. As a coach myself, I am a firm believer in the importance of coaching, but it had been some years since I had had a coach of my own. You are now holding this book in your hands as a result of the guidance and accountability of my amazing coach. The decision to hire a coach helped me get intentional; I've had a long list of development goals sitting on the back burner for the last five years that are now getting accomplished because of the deliberate focus she helped me achieve. It's so easy as leaders to get caught up in the day-to-day demands and get sidetracked from being strategic in the way we get work done.

Today, we are focusing on increasing our levels of **intentionality**.

WHAT IS INTENTIONALITY?

Intentionality is being deliberate and acting on purpose. Leaders strong in this skill have a clear vision for the outcomes they want to achieve, whether for their organizations, their teams, a particular meeting, or their own leadership development. They are deliberate about having a strategy, focusing their efforts, and managing any distractions. In the context of emotional intelligence at work, cultivating intentionality means having plans to achieve our goals and taking consistent actions until those goals are complete.

BENEFITS OF INTENTIONALITY

This self-management skill helps us to *actually* follow through on achieving our desired goals and aspirations. When a leader exhibits intentionality, it also provides great clarity for their team, improving their ability to be focused and productive.

One aspect of intentionality that is especially challenging for leaders is capacity management, the ability to manage one's time and energy in a sustainable way. More than ever, today's leaders are on the cusp of burnout. Today's reading will focus on cultivating this aspect of intentionality so you can finally achieve your most important goals *and* maintain your sanity.

SYMPTOMS THAT YOU MAY NEED TO BUILD YOUR SKILL SET IN INTENTIONALITY

- Your team is unclear about their goals and priorities.
- If you do set strategic goals for your organization or team, they carry over year after year instead of getting completed in a timely manner.
- You find yourself getting easily distracted or sidetracked from getting things done.

KATHERINE, VP OF MARKETING, ADVERTISING AGENCY

After being promoted to her dream job as VP, my client Katherine realized that her current way of operating would not be sustainable for long. She had come to believe that constant exhaustion and overwhelm were just part of leadership. That had always been the model her own leaders had exhibited, and this gave her mixed feelings about moving up in the company. While she was excited about her new position, she feared it would overtake her both professionally and personally and compromise her value of having a good work/life balance.

When we don't manage our capacities, we aren't able to show up as our best selves, and things begin to fall through the cracks with our teams. Some telltale signs that we may be out of sync include becoming less accessible to the people who need us, not having the energy to have the challenging or important conversations, not prioritizing development and strategic planning, and neglecting to take vacations and enjoy life outside of work. This puts us in a kind of survival mode, with only the ability to focus on the immediate needs of the day. Nearly every leader I know (including me!) has struggled with capacity management. Unaddressed, this begins to have a trickle-down effect, influencing team morale, alignment, and performance—among many other things!

The first area for improvement Katherine and I identified was that the main components for the year (meetings, events, conferences, travel, and vacations) needed to be calendared. It's very important to calendar vacations ahead of time! Next, we added both small and big project deadlines to Katherine's calendar and worked backward to map out the time and resources needed to complete them. Katherine rated the energy and time required for each item on a scale of 1 to 5 so we could place items strategically to prevent burnout. Then we did what I call a margin audit. Was there space in her calendar for the unexpected? (Margin is intentional unscheduled time, such as space between meetings in case they run over or you need time to prepare and availability to meet with team members to have important conversations as they come up.) Finally, we made a list of tasks Katherine could delegate. We noted who she could delegate those tasks to and made a plan for training those people. We revisited her calendar monthly and made adjustments as needed.

Three years later, Katherine is accomplishing more than ever, but without burnout and overwhelm. She continues to feel empowered and in control over her calendar. As a result, she actually has the potential to stretch her capacity further if needed as her role continues to expand. Small tweaks truly make a difference.

Katherine's choice to be intentional in capacity management has enabled her to not only perform well but also have time and space to nurture the same in her team. She is also breaking mindsets of those she leads, modeling that burnout and overwhelm do not have to be synonymous with leadership!

ACTION STEP

Want to get results like Katherine's? Here's what you can do.
(Choose one or both of the following options.)

Eat the Frog

Personal and professional development expert Brian Tracy developed a strategy for getting intentional called "Eat That Frog." It works like this: In preparing for your workday tomorrow, identify your most important and challenging task that needs to get done. Do that task *first*, before anything else. This starts your day off with a sense of accomplishment and momentum toward achieving your most important goals. Try incorporating the "Eat That Frog" technique into your daily work planning.

Identify Your Big 3

Leadership author Michael Hyatt suggests consistently identifying your "Big 3," which are three important goals and the tasks necessary to complete them. Use the prompts below to complete your Big 3 for various different time periods in your life.

- What is your Big 3 for the **year**?
- What is your Big 3 for the **quarter**?
- What is your Big 3 for this **month**?
- What is your Big 3 for **today**?

Day 7

Being a Leader of Action

You can't build a reputation on what you are going to do.

— ATTRIBUTED TO HENRY FORD

One of my favorite movies of 2023 was *Air*, the story of how a then-struggling Nike secured a coveted partnership with NBA player Michael Jordan and created the infamous Air Jordan shoes. The most compelling part of the story for me was watching the innovative and unprecedented actions of Sonny Vaccaro, a sports marketing executive for Nike. Originally, Jordan had planned to sign a deal with either Adidas or Converse. Vaccaro could have accepted Jordan's plans, but instead he took the initiative to facilitate one of the most infamous partnerships in sports history. To lure Jordan to Nike, Vaccaro proposed a signature shoe line to promote Jordan as a stand-alone star. He also broke NBA rules by designing the shoes in the Chicago Bulls colors, which was a violation of the league's uniform policies at the time. He was willing to pay thousands of dollars in fines per game to secure Jordan's commitment. Later, when Jordan agreed to sign with Nike, Vaccaro also honored his request to make a percentage on each shoe sold, which had never been done before. The sales goal for Air Jordans was set at $3 million for the first year, but sales exceeded everyone's expectations, bringing in $126 million that year.

Vaccaro is an extraordinary example of leadership that took initiative and moved around perceived limitations to deliver results. He could've let the influence of bigger brands intimidate him or the rules of the NBA restrict his shoe design, but instead he found a way to make Nike stand out. The partnership with Jordan help propel Nike to become the successful and well-known brand that it is today.

Today, we are focusing on increasing our levels of **initiative and bias for action**.

WHAT IS INITIATIVE AND BIAS FOR ACTION?

Like other self-management skills, initiative and bias for action—which, as the name suggests, involves doing things without being told and choosing to favor taking action over staying in a place of stasis—helps us nurture our sense of self-leadership and take personal responsibility for our lives. Essentially, it's a "can-do" attitude and a belief in the values of being proactive and persistent. It's finding opportunity amid challenges and navigating around roadblocks. In the context of emotional intelligence at work, it's not letting our emotions get in the way of taking necessary actions and not getting caught up in paralysis by analysis.

BENEFITS OF INITIATIVE AND BIAS FOR ACTION

Leaders strong in this skill are proactive in creating the circumstances they desire rather than waiting for circumstances to change. They continuously pursue new opportunities and know how to effectively mobilize the efforts of their teams and maneuver around obstacles. They are people of action, inspiring their organizations to take risks and continuously grow.

SYMPTOMS THAT YOU MAY NEED TO BUILD YOUR SKILL SET IN INITIATIVE AND BIAS FOR ACTION

- You often find yourself procrastinating and falling behind.
- You have a tendency not to plan ahead, causing your team to have to rush to complete work at the last minute.
- You wait until external circumstances force you to act rather than taking a proactive approach.

JORGE, ASSOCIATE, ENGINEERING FIRM

Jorge is a bright and technically skilled engineer who moved his way up to senior-level leadership because of his strong relationships with clients and his ability to juggle multiple projects at once. After many years in the industry, Jorge desired to move up to the executive level of leadership and become a partner. While his technical abilities were strong, he received lower scores in a couple of key areas on his annual performance reviews. Because of this, he was not able to move to the next level.

Jorge received three main pieces of feedback: (1) his

projects were barely meeting deadlines and important details were falling through the cracks, (2) he often came unprepared for meetings with his team and peers, and (3) some of his projects were losing money. When we went over this feedback together, Jorge admitted that all these areas needed attention, but his tendency was to blame other people and circumstances, leaving him feeling disempowered and defeated.

He felt that he didn't have enough staff on his projects to meet deadlines, that the company was overworking him to the point that he did not have time to prepare for meetings, and that he had received poor mentorship regarding how to evaluate and track project profitability. Unlike someone strong in initiative and bias for action, Jorge felt he had to wait for the people and circumstances around him to change before there could be any improvement.

I encouraged Jorge to look at each area in which he was struggling and identify all the actions he could take independently of others to improve the outcomes in those areas. In doing so, we discovered there was a lot more he could do than he realized. Jorge had the tendency to say yes to every project that came in without evaluating his team's capacity to deliver. He also was not coming prepared to meetings that provided opportunities to staff his projects and lay out project plans for his team. He realized that much of what was leading him to feel overworked was self-imposed and not coming from pressure from his company. In terms of mentorship, I encouraged him to identify the people who were strong in the skills he needed to develop for promotion and pursue them for guidance instead of just relying upon his immediate boss for mentorship or waiting for others to offer to mentor him. Once we identified ways that Jorge could take more initiative and action, he immediately began to feel empowered.

Over the course of the next couple of months, Jorge took consistent actions around the areas where he needed to improve, and things began to change. He was more intentional about which projects he took on, took time to identify staffing needs prior to meetings and began asking for what he needed, created work plans for his team, and met with several different mentors to gain the skills he needed for the promotion he was looking for. With more margin in his schedule, Jorge was also freed up to be more strategic overall, both to take on new opportunities and find ways around previously perceived "obstacles." In his recent review, Jorge's feedback improved dramatically. As a result, he is now in the pool for consideration for promotion during the next round.

ACTION STEP

Want to get results like Jorge's? Here's what you can do.

Action Audit

Reflect on the following three questions. If you want to take things a step further, have three people on your team also answer these questions about you, and compare your answers with theirs to ensure accurate self-awareness.

1. What is your current track record for delivering on your promises and deadlines?
2. Do you have good systems for mobilizing others and managing their work?
3. Is there margin in your schedule to be strategic for development and acting on opportunities?

Next, identify one action you can take in each area to improve outcomes.

Day 8
Rise Above It

Mastering the art of resilience does much more than restore you to who you once thought you were. Rather, you emerge from the experience transformed into a truer expression of who you were really meant to be.

— CAROL ORSBORN

I f there is one event in recent history that challenged every leader's resilience, it was the outbreak of the COVID-19 virus. As a leadership coach, I found myself in a new experience: helping leaders navigate circumstances that were unprecedented and unfamiliar to all of us. My coaching team had to fall back on principles learned through collective experiences navigating past crises. In doing so, we were reminded that half the battle is how you choose to interpret the "crisis"; the other is how you communicate about it and navigate it with your team. We got to witness amazing leadership in the face of challenges as companies pivoted to remote work, found innovative ways of delivering products and services, and found new markets to serve when business from longtime clients dried up.

The majority of the organizations we work with are actually stronger and more profitable now than they were before COVID-19. How is that possible? It's the result of the courage and tenacity of strong leadership.

Today, we are focusing on increasing our levels of **resilience**.

WHAT IS RESILIENCE?

Resilience is a self-management skill that helps us to address challenges in an empowering way; it's the ability to bounce back from setbacks and continue forward. In the context of emotional intelligence at work, cultivating resilience means remaining positive and flexible in the face of challenges and perceived failures rather than giving in to feelings of defeat and getting stuck.

BENEFITS OF RESILIENCE

Leaders strong in this skill create teams that are also highly resilient, as they model several key behaviors. Resilient leaders view setbacks as temporary and "failures" as opportunities for growth. They are optimistic and communicate in ways that inspire confidence, creativity, and perseverance in their teams.

SYMPTOMS THAT YOU MAY NEED TO BUILD YOUR SKILL SET IN RESILIENCE

- Your first response when your team experiences challenges is stress and overwhelm.

- You take "failure" hard instead of seeing it as a learning experience.
- You assume you must handle challenges on your own instead of getting help and ideas from others.

JENNA, OWNER, MEDICAL CLINIC

When I think of the skill of resilience, I immediately think of my client Jenna. She owns a successful medical practice. During one of our coaching sessions, she shared a horrifying discovery: Her operations person had been embezzling hundreds of thousands of dollars from the business. Not only was this a professional betrayal, but it was also a personal one that affected the entire team, as they all shared a close relationship with this person. The team had worked hard to build a successful practice, and now it was clear why the volume of patients did not match the level of income the practice was bringing in. The loss was also difficult on a practical level—the operations person had been a key employee who oversaw the clinic's back-end systems.

The fallout of a betrayal of this magnitude and its impact on the business and team could be overwhelming for any leader. In coaching, I suggested that Jenna articulate to me what kind of leader she wanted to be as she navigated the situation. I asked her to share what she envisioned a stronger team and a more profitable business would look like a year in the future. I asked her if she felt she could forecast victory versus defeat to her team in the way she communicated. I asked her if she led in such a way that this "crisis" could be viewed as an opportunity to make the business better and help her team grow closer. This exercise was an amazing one to witness, as Jenna began articulating her vision for the business and the leadership philosophy that would get her team there.

Just a couple months later, Jenna shared some of the unexpected opportunities that had surfaced as a result of the "crisis." During the investigation, it was discovered that many of the processes and systems the former operations person had set up had been inefficient. Cleaning up these systems would profoundly affect the business. Jenna also found unexpected resources in the form of a family member who offered to take over finances and profit projections. She trusted this person completely, and he was actually exceptionally more skilled than the operations person had been! No matter how things look, "crisis" always comes with opportunities if you are open to seeing them and willing to search them out. Some are obvious and some are more subtle, but they are there. If you can position yourself to look for them, that mindset will set you on a path to be resilient.

Jenna also created a closer bond with her team. She wanted to be known as both a transparent and caring leader, and she kept that desire front of mind in all her communication and interactions with her team.

Jenna's team had to temporarily take on more responsibilities, but they are fully committed to Jenna, the patients, and the business's success. They all want to see the vision Jenna articulated for the future realized. And, because the business has a resilient leader like Jenna at the helm, I know this vision *will* be realized!

Resilience is one of those leadership skills that cannot be learned from a course or book; it has to be built through experiencing real-life challenges and leading through them in a resilient way. Becoming a resilient leader strengthens your confidence as a leader and equips you to be a leader who inspires others. It's a magnetic strength that makes people want to follow you.

ACTION STEP

Want to get results like Jenna's? Here's what you can do.

Letter to Future You Exercise

Write a letter to your future self. Imagine yourself past the current "crisis" and settled into a new season of success. Describe exactly what things look like resolved and functioning at their best (you can use the questions I posed to Jenna above as a guide to craft your letter). If you are not currently facing a crisis, describe how you will get past a future crisis.

Bonus Action: Learn from Someone You Admire

If you want to take things a step further, research or read a biography about someone you deeply admire. Most successful people have had a series of "crises" that they have had to overcome through resilience. Take note of the qualities the person you research used to handle their own crises, and incorporate those qualities into your situation.

Day 9
Take Back Control

Do not let what you cannot do interfere with what you can do.

— JOHN WOODEN

My coach said it offhandedly, but her words stuck with me: "Overwhelm is a choice." Considering the list of legitimate stressors I had just laid out for her, it felt like a cold reaction at first, but later, it became an empowering mantra I have been able to live out with much greater "stressors" than I described to her at that time.

Many of us have heard the saying that 10 percent of life is what happens to you and 90 percent is how you react. My own journey with managing stress and coaching leaders to do the same has taught me that often, how we react to stress is a learned response. This explains why, when a child falls, they look at their parent's reaction and mirror it back. It's why we look at the faces of flight attendants when we hit turbulence. If they are not worried, maybe there is not a reason for us to be.

When you choose to look at overwhelm as a choice, it gives you the opportunity to focus your actions on the things you can control and recognize the things you can't. Choices to reduce or eliminate certain stressors become illuminated, and you can become empowered again, rather than feeling like a victim of circumstance. Like the child looks to their parent or the passenger looks to the flight attendant, our teams are looking to us as leaders to identify how to respond to challenges. We have the unique opportunity to create teams and cultures that can continue to thrive under stress.

Today, we are focusing on increasing our levels of **stress management**.

WHAT IS STRESS MANAGEMENT?

Stress management is the ability the cope with stress and reduce its negative effects. This self-management skill helps us show up well, regardless of our circumstances, and maintain positive relationships with others. In the context of emotional intelligence at work, cultivating stress management means being able to work calmly under stress and pressure.

BENEFITS OF STRESS MANAGEMENT

Leaders strong in this skill recognize that stress is inevitable, but they also believe they can manage their responses to it. They exercise influence over stressful situations by taking actions around the things they can control and letting go of the things they can't. They also maintain their composure when met with unfavorable reactions and behavior from others. Leaders strong in stress management influence their teams in many positive ways—a less stressed leader means a less stressed team that is more creative and productive! These leaders are also able to be more present, accessible, and tuned in to the needs of their teams. Unmanaged stress tends to make us very self-focused and creates a barrier in our relationships with others.

SYMPTOMS THAT YOU MAY NEED TO BUILD YOUR SKILL SET IN STRESS MANAGEMENT

- You are chronically sick and don't make time for rest, good nutrition, and exercise.
- You are often in survival mode, blaming your circumstances for how you feel instead of feeling empowered to manage your reactions and boundaries.
- You tend to do work yourself that could be delegated to others on your team.

JENIFER, DIRECTOR OF PEOPLE OPERATIONS, ARCHITECTURAL FIRM

The job of the HR professional is a demanding one, not only because the focus of their work is navigating interpersonal complexities within a variety of contexts, but also because they're doing so in a way that meets ever-changing legal and regulatory requirements. In recent years, I have had a significant influx of HR leaders reach out for coaching, both to manage their own stress and to acquire tools to support leaders at every level of their organizations to do the same.

When I met Jenifer, she had just stepped into her role as director of people operations, a role created specifically for her. The role hadn't existed before, so she was experiencing stress from pioneering a new position and carrying out the long list of responsibilities. Because people within her organization had never had anyone in that position before, they were coming to her with every question from "Who is supposed to refill the paper towels in the bathroom?" to "What do I do if I am being harassed by someone on my team?" Her office was also close to a communal area, so she was getting a constant flow of people dropping in unexpectedly to talk with her. Those constant interruptions prevented her from focusing and getting her most time-sensitive work done.

Jenifer began to feel stressed, and her focus became divided when she was talking to people. This earned her an unfavorable reputation; people perceived her as disengaged and not very personable. She was disheartened by this perception, but she was not sure what to do.

The first exercise I took her through is what I call the "Control/Can't Control" exercise. I had her take out a piece of paper and create two columns. In one column, she listed the things she could control in the situation, and in the other, she listed the things she couldn't. Some of the things she listed in the "Control" column included having a clear role description and communicating that to staff so they knew what to go to her for, creating a system for scheduling appointments with her, blocking out time every day to shut her door to work on time-sensitive tasks (we crafted good communication around this so that the staff knew the tasks she was completing were organization-wide and in service to them), and having an open office hour each day where people could drop in and ask questions without appointments. Then she made a list of the things that she couldn't control, which ended up being pretty short. With this new sense of clarity about what she could and couldn't control, Jenifer immediately felt less stressed and more empowered to take action.

Jenifer and I collaborated to identify the actions she could take over the next month, three months, and six months. At the six-month mark, Jenifer expressed that her stress level had gone from a 10 to a 3. Her team appreciated the clarity and recognized that the boundaries and structures she had put in place were in service to them. Jenifer is now thriving in her role and was recently promoted to an executive-level position. As her coach, I couldn't be prouder to see her modeling a new way of working to her entire organization.

ACTION STEP

Want to get results like Jenifer's? Here's what you can do.

"Control/Can't Control" Exercise

Create a document and, at the top of the page, describe the situation causing you the most stress. In the first column, make a list of the things about the situation that you can control. In the second column, make a list of the things you can't control. Take the list of things you can control and generate an action list. What actions can you take over the next month, three months, and six months to address your "Can Control" items? Focus your energy there. Then make every effort to let go of the things on the "Can't Control" list.

Day 10
Getting Creative

No matter what you are currently able to do, creativity can make you capable of more.

— JOHN C. MAXWELL

One of the best movies I watched this year was *Flamin' Hot*, the inspiring true story of Richard Montañez, a janitor at Frito-Lay, whose creative idea helped revolutionize the snack industry. Drawing from his Mexican heritage, Montañez developed the flavoring for Flamin' Hot Cheetos that became a phenomenon! Not only did this idea open a new cultural market for the company, it allowed Montañez to be recognized as a leader; he moved up the ranks at Frito-Lay from janitor to VP of multicultural sales. As Montañez's story shows, innovation can come from the most unlikely of places and is a quality of leaders who can build companies *and* create sustainable and timeless success.

Today, we are focusing on increasing our levels of **creativity and innovation.**

WHAT IS CREATIVITY AND INNOVATION?

This self-management skill has two components: creativity, which is the generation of original ideas, and innovation, which is the ability to take those ideas and translate them into tangible solutions, such as products or services. In the context of emotional intelligence at work, cultivating creativity and innovation means actively pursuing new ideas and approaches.

BENEFITS OF CREATIVITY AND INNOVATION

Leaders strong in this skill create teams that are flexible, adaptable, and willing to take thoughtful risks for long-term rewards. They create learning cultures that aren't afraid to "fail," which enables them to learn the lessons necessary for eventual success. They regularly brainstorm with their teams, asking good questions that help bring out great ideas. As a result, they create teams that are highly engaged, knowing their ideas and contributions are valued and rewarded.

SYMPTOMS THAT YOU MAY NEED TO BUILD YOUR SKILL SET IN CREATIVITY AND INNOVATION

- You find yourself immediately dismissing your team's new or different ideas.
- You tend to be slow to implement the necessary changes that are best for your organization in the long run.
- You don't take vacations or you have given up hobbies you enjoy in favor of work, even though both of these things are experiences that give you the space to be creative.

LEADERS AT ALL LEVELS IN VARIOUS INDUSTRIES

I taught a creativity and innovation in leadership course at the graduate level for many years. All of my students were at various levels of leadership in their organizations and wished to hone their skills in this area. In today's reading, I'll share the tools that helped them the most.

People often ask if leaders are born or made, and a similar question can be asked about creativity: Are people born creative, or can you become creative? The first thing to clarify is what being creative really means. Often, being creative gets confused with being artistic, which includes things like painting and the arts. Creativity is something I believe everyone is born with to varying degrees. If you've traveled on a budget or found a way to get your kid to eat their vegetables, you are creative. Whatever your starting point, though, you have room to build on your skill set. Creativity and innovation is a key differentiator between leaders and managers, as leaders are change agents.

In my experience, I find that leaders are often so overwhelmed with the demands of their roles that they don't feel like they have the headspace and energy to think creatively. They continue doing things the way they have always been done because there is no margin in their schedules for thinking beyond the day-to-day. Today, between work and home life, leaders are busier than ever. But there were three key tools that I saw make a profound impact on my students' ability to develop their creative muscles. These are also tools I later used with executives. Both groups saw the same great results. (The first two tools are shared in Mark Bryan, Julia Cameron, and Catherine Allen's book *The Artist's Way at Work: Riding the Dragon.*)

The first tool is morning pages. These are done first thing

in the morning by writing continuously until you have filled three full pages. This brain dump allows you to get the clutter out of your mind at the start of your day so that you can get the clarity necessary to prioritize. Morning pages also serve as a place to process anything that is bothering you and write down things you don't want to forget. My students who completed morning pages at least three times a week reported greater productivity and clarity and more space for creative ideas and problem-solving.

The second tool is time-outs, setting aside an hour a week to do something you truly enjoy—whether that's surfing or reading a novel—without any sense of responsibility. Creative ideas often come when the pressure to come up with an idea is removed and you are focused on something else. My students who did time-outs weekly reported less stress, a renewed energy for their work, and an increase in the number of ideas and solutions that came to them spontaneously while they did things they enjoyed.

A third tool is the common object exercise, which I learned in one of my college classes. If you want to get the creative juices flowing, place a common object like a coffee mug in front of you and come up with as many uses for the mug beyond the obvious as you can. You can also do this exercise at the beginning of a team meeting to prime the pump before a work-related brainstorming session. My students who did the common object exercise before brainstorming sessions found there to be greater ease and flow to generating ideas.

Wherever you currently are, these tools are guaranteed to build or strengthen your creative muscle.

ACTION STEP

Want to get results like my students'? Here's what you can do.

(Choose one or more of the following options.)

Morning Pages

Start doing morning pages a couple of days a week. Julia Cameron, who originally created the exercise, recommends refraining from rereading what you have written, at least for a time.[1] My recommendation is that you wait at least a month if you choose to revisit them. I have found it helpful to review with a highlighter in hand to mark themes and key learnings. In reflecting, you may rediscover your values and what's important to you, which could prompt necessary changes. You may also discover that solutions to problems surfaced when you processed your challenges through writing. These are just a couple of examples of the benefits I have seen.

Time-Out

Put one hour on your calendar every week to do something you can get lost in and enjoy. At the end of your time, reflect on your stress levels and any ideas, clarity, or both that have come from that time.

Common Object Exercise

Do this exercise at the start of a brainstorming meeting.

---

1. Julia Cameron, *The Artist's Way: A Spiritual Path to Higher Creativity* (Jeremy P. Tarcher/Putnam, 1992), 10.

After the meeting, reflect on how it helped the group get into a creative flow.

Bonus Action: The Artist's Way at Work

Read *The Artist's Way at Work* by Bryan, Cameron, and Allen. Complete any of the exercises throughout the book that resonate with you. After reading, reflect on how the exercises have helped you to become more creative.

Day 11
Managing Up

I don't want to be at the mercy of my emotions. I want to use them, to enjoy them, and to dominate them.

— OSCAR WILDE

When I first began to delve into the world of emotional intelligence, I came across a quote by Daniel Goleman that really struck me. He said that "Out of control emotions can make smart people stupid."[1] When I read this, I laughed out loud because he put into words what I had experienced firsthand from the leadership I was under early in my career. My first three jobs out of college were in a variety of industries: entertainment, nonprofit, and international community development. In each of those jobs, I had had leaders who were extremely intelligent and competent in their roles, but who didn't have mastery over their emotions. While people had respect for

---

1. Goleman, *Working with Emotional Intelligence*, 22.

them professionally, having personal trust in them was a challenge. These experiences were why I got into the field of leadership development. I wanted to learn how to help leaders get equipped not only technically but also relationally. While technical competence gets you promoted into leadership, it's the relational skills like the ability to manage your emotions that engender the trust, loyalty, and engagement that every leader is seeking.

Today, we're again working on increasing our levels of **behavioral self-control**.

WHAT IS BEHAVIORAL SELF-CONTROL?

You may remember that leaders strong in this skill are great about impulse control, even in the face of challenges. On day 4, we talked about how to identify and address our hot buttons so that we don't lose control in the workplace. Today we will take a different angle and focus on mastering our emotions when managing up (developing a positive and productive relationship with those who oversee us). When we talk about the idea of being able to lead anyone, that also applies to being able to sometimes lead those who lead us. Depending on your current level of leadership, who leads you will differ, but it's ultimately who you are accountable to (for example, it could include a board of directors). Managing up includes seeking to understand what those who lead you value and want to achieve, knowing how best to communicate with them, anticipating their needs, and then taking actions that support those things. Similar to gaining influence with the team you lead, it's important to not just look to your own interests but also look to the interests of those who lead you to create a reciprocal dynamic in the relationship. Your oversight holds a lot of decision-making power over your career opportunities and progression, so learning to master your emotions when you get triggered will allow you to maintain your influence, especially over outcomes that matter to you.

BENEFITS OF BEHAVIORAL SELF-CONTROL

Within the context of managing up, one of the primary benefits of keeping your cool is the trust that is cultivated between you and your leader. Rarely do people try to understand the weight their leader is carrying or what goes into the decisions they make, especially when things don't go their way. No matter how you feel about those decisions—or your leader themself—managing up can be a great way to maintain positive relationships, cultivate a powerful workplace reputation, and place yourself in a position to advocate for your needs when the time is right.

SYMPTOMS THAT YOU MAY NEED TO BUILD YOUR SKILL SET IN BEHAVIORAL SELF-CONTROL

- You find yourself making assumptions about leadership's decisions without knowing all the facts.
- You tend to focus on how your leader can support you but aren't as intentional in seeking ways you can support your leader.
- You sometimes lose your cool when your leader makes a decision that you don't agree with.

LAURA, SENIOR ASSOCIATE, ARCHITECTURAL FIRM

My client Laura is a shining example of someone who was willing to temper her emotions in the short-term for a significant long-term gain. Laura worked her way up into leadership in an industry with few women at that level. She brought a lot of interesting work into the firm and was a beloved leader. She brought something different to the firm beyond technical expertise—she helped the firm realize the importance of nurturing and developing its people, created better processes for clear communication, and introduced a pathway for career progression. Her initiatives alone significantly increased the firm's retention rates.

Her career goals included being promoted to partner. There weren't any female partners yet, and she was confident she could bring value to the team and create a pathway for more women within the organization to pursue higher levels of leadership.

Her performance reviews exceeded the requirements to move to the next level. When Laura reached out for coaching, she was looking for support in how to find her voice among an established group and optimize her opportunities for promotion.

During the time for annual reviews and promotions, Laura submitted her name for consideration to become a partner and receive a pay raise. When she met with her boss, she was given another shining review and a portion of the pay raise she had requested. Her boss told her that the promotion couldn't be granted yet, but he would work on it. Laura kept her cool in the moment, but during our next coaching session, she expressed her disappointment and anger. She was ready to quit. I happened to know her boss well and knew he was a fair and thoughtful person who very much wanted more diversity in the senior leadership team, so I knew there had to be more to the story.

When coaching people to manage up, I ask them to put themselves in their boss's shoes and to identify what their greatest concerns might be—what keeps them up at night. It's easy to only see things from your own point of view instead of recognizing the variety of factors a higher-level leader is considering when making decisions, things that you may not know about. When I noted this to Laura, she softened and shared that she was aware her boss had a lot of political "hoops to jump through" to do anything new. I emphasized to Laura how important managing her emotions would be and reminded her to keep her big-picture goals in mind. I suggested she send her boss an email thanking him for the pay raise and requesting a follow-up meeting to get clarity about her career path moving forward. I encouraged her to take the high road and not let her emotions get the best of her.

Laura met with her boss and expressed her gratitude and disappointment. She acknowledged that there may have been considerations she was unaware of that had gone into the decision, but she told her boss that she wanted to know what her path forward could look like. She needed the information so that she could make decisions going forward. Her boss shared that he wanted the current partner team to embrace her and needed time to iron out some old school dynamics. He hoped she could give him some time, but he also understood if she couldn't. Laura offered to put her contributions into a document he could share with the team. In the meantime, Laura continued to have a good attitude and bring a lot of value while keeping her options open in case she decided to move on.

Within nine months, Laura's boss came back to her and

made her a partner designee for the next year with a pay raise and full backing from everyone on the team.

I often think about how things might have been different if Laura had let her emotions master her instead of choosing to master them.

ACTION STEP

Want to get results like Laura's? Here's what you can do.

Change the Story, Take 2

Repeat the Change the Story exercise from day 4. As a refresher, here it is again:

Hot Button → Thought → Feeling → Reaction

- What is a hot button you want to address?
- What is the thought or story you have about this trigger?
- What feeling do you have in response to that thought or story?
- What is your current reaction?

Now ask yourself...

- Am I certain this story is true? What can I do to get clarity?
- What is a new story that will lead to a different feeling?
- How does this information affect what I am now feeling?
- What will my response be going forward?

Part III

Social Awareness

The first half of the book focused on leading ourselves well by increasing our skills in self-awareness and self-management. Our journey to lead anyone starts with being able to lead ourselves first. The strength of our self-leadership has a direct impact on our ability to lead others. Equal in importance is our relationships with others because people are more likely to follow someone they feel connected to. The second half of this book will focus on the relationship-building skill set needed to lead anyone.

The third core competency of leading with emotional intelligence is social awareness. People high in social awareness are other-focused. They can accurately read people, pick up on others' emotions, and discern social cues. They are able to see things from another's perspective and hold space for that, even if they disagree.

Social awareness gives you insights for building relationships and connections with those you lead. People don't follow a title; they follow a person. The greater the connection you have with your team, the greater the influence you will have.

In this section, we will cover three core skills to help you increase your social awareness:

1. Empathy
2. Organizational awareness
3. Service orientation

When we are managing instead of leading, our style can get very transactional, focusing solely on task accomplishment. Leading recognizes that work gets done *through* people, so the quality of our relationship with our team matters. Taking the time to focus on improving your relationship with your team is actually a win-win: You'll find that as your connection with your team grows stronger, more gets done.

Day 12
Get Curious

Maturity begins to grow when you can sense your concern for others outweighs your concern for yourself.

— JOHN MACNAUGHTON

We have all heard of the golden rule, "Treat others as you would like them to treat you," but have you heard of the platinum rule? It states that we should "treat others as *they* want to be treated." Both of these principles are rooted in empathy, as they require us to consider others' perspectives and feelings. Many leaders shy away from the topic of empathy, perceiving it to be a touchy-feely trait irrelevant to business. But, if you think of it from a business perspective, we use "empathy" to understand what our customers need and want and adjust our approach to meet those things. It's the same with our teams: people who feel seen and heard are much more likely to feel connected to us as their leaders. Those relationships then have the potential to engender increases in loyalty and retention.

Today, we are focusing on increasing our levels of **empathy**.

WHAT IS EMPATHY?

Like our other social awareness skills, empathy helps us connect with other people. You may already be familiar with the concept of empathy from your day-to-day life—it's the ability to share and understand the feelings of those around us—but in the context of emotional intelligence at work, cultivating empathy means acting from a place of curiosity, patience, and kindness rather than a place of assumptions and judgment.

BENEFITS OF EMPATHY

Leaders strong in this skill are able to establish strong connections with people, even people very different from themselves. They can detect others' emotional cues and adjust their approach in response. They also have the ability to see things from alternate perspectives and take an interest in how others think and feel about things. In my experience, empathy is one of the most misunderstood and underused leadership superpowers.

SYMPTOMS THAT YOU MAY NEED TO BUILD YOUR SKILL SET IN EMPATHY

- You find yourself automatically judging others as weak or complainers when they express struggles you can't relate to.

- You feel uncomfortable listening to people express emotion and find yourself quickly going into problem-solving mode.
- You find yourself getting defensive and arguing your point if someone has a different perspective rather than trying to understand them.

TOM, CEO, CONSULTING FIRM

When I challenged my type A, no-nonsense client Tom to begin incorporating more empathy into the way he led, he gained the ease of influence and respect he had always desired with his team.

Tom has a commanding and assertive presence. He is incredibly smart and has an amazing capacity to get done in a day what takes most people a week. When I met Tom for the first time, I was immediately struck by his passionate energy. He told me he was struggling with an underperforming team, which concerned him as he was nearing retirement. He didn't want to retire until he was assured he could confidently hand off his responsibilities to his team. Tom shared some examples of underperformance and how he addressed them. It very quickly became clear to me that Tom's passionate energy could be misdirected into some intimidating and harsh approaches. As former military, he was used to the command-and-control style of leading, but that wasn't working for his team.

I got Tom's permission to do a series of short interviews with each member of his executive team, and my suspicions about Tom's approach were confirmed. Various leaders on his team recalled being humiliated in front of the team, being called names, and receiving cutting remarks on a regular basis. They unanimously said that his approach shut the team down and was creating a pressure that was causing more mistakes to be made.

Tom was initially defensive when he heard this feedback. "If they were doing their jobs, I wouldn't have to lay into them so hard." Despite his defense, though, he was desperate to get things in order so he could retire.

I introduced him to the idea of taking a more empathetic approach. We started by identifying his hot buttons (see day 1). Then Tom identified a situation he needed to address: Jesse, one of the leaders on his team, had announced that he would be stepping down from presenting at conferences. This triggered Tom because it meant that those engagements would have to be filled by an already overextended team. Tom assumed that Jesse was being selfish and didn't care about how his decision would impact the team.

I encouraged Tom to do an empathy experiment instead of confronting Jesse in his usual way. I find that often, when a person needs to cultivate empathy, it helps to stop, get calm, and get curious about the situation. One quality of empathy is the ability to be curious and ask questions instead of making assumptions. Where is the other person coming from? How are they feeling? How can you help in a way you might not have thought of before? In Tom's case, I thought it was important that he find out why Jesse had stepped down, if Jesse was comfortable sharing.

Tom learned that Jesse felt that he was underperforming based on the feedback he had received from Tom and the team. Jesse wanted to continue to present, but he didn't want to be a burden or embarrassment to the team. Tom realized the impact of his words and was able to empathize with how Jesse was feeling. This opened up the opportunity for Tom to mentor Jesse in presenting without removing him. It was a win-win!

After experiencing such a different outcome, Tom was

completely on board with continuing to experiment with an empathetic approach. One year later, Tom's team describes him as someone who truly cares about them and has their back. The team's performance issues? Resolved. And what is Tom doing now? Enjoying his retirement!

ACTION STEP

Want to get results like Tom's? Here's what you can do.

Empathy Reflection

Watch Brené Brown's animated video on empathy (https://brenebrown.com/videos/rsa-short-empathy/). This short video helps demystify what empathy is. After watching, write down what you learned about what it is and isn't.

Empathy Experiment

Conduct your own empathy experiment. Choose a situation with someone you find challenging to connect with. Instead of making negative assumptions, approach them in a calm and curious way to learn about their perspective. Acknowledge their thoughts and feelings. How has learning this information illuminated a path forward?

Day 13
Cracking the
Culture Code

There is a voice that doesn't use words. Listen.

— ANONYMOUS

What do investigators, poker players, and psychologists have in common? If they are really good at their jobs, they have the ability to read people and situations well. They can tell if someone is bluffing or telling the truth by referencing subtle signals in their eyes and body language. They have the ability to pick up on things others can't see, allowing those cues to influence their desired outcomes. In the same way, standout leaders have the ability to read and decode the subtle and unspoken norms of their organizations.

Today, we are focusing on increasing our levels of **organizational awareness**.

WHAT IS ORGANIZATIONAL AWARENESS?

Organizational awareness is the ability to accurately read the internal dynamics within an organization—observing the unspoken rules, identifying who the influencers are, and picking up on the emotional currents of the group. In the context of emotional intelligence at work, cultivating organizational awareness means being able to gather tangible and intangible data. It's empathy on an organizational scale.

BENEFITS OF ORGANIZATIONAL AWARENESS

Leaders strong in this skill have a good pulse on how people think and feel, not only on their teams but also in their organizations as a whole. They have informal conversations with others to get their input, thoughts, and feelings on a regular basis. They use this information to inform effective strategies and decisions. They are able to build coalitions with key influencers to support organizational development and change. They are also skilled in identifying the unspoken cultural norms that support or undermine desired outcomes.

SYMPTOMS THAT YOU MAY NEED TO BUILD YOUR SKILL SET IN ORGANIZATIONAL AWARENESS

- You are not sure who to go to to get things done in your workplace, and when you try to collaborate with others, you are often met with indifference or resistance.
- You don't have strong relationships with those who have influence within your organization, and, other than immediate leadership, you're not sure who your company's strongest influencers are.

- You find that the strategies you try to implement rarely get much, if any, buy-in, and you can't figure out why.

JIM, CEO, WEALTH MANAGEMENT COMPANY

When Jim reached out for coaching, he was feeling unable to move initiatives forward within his executive leadership team. He knew each member was fully competent in their role and was capable of implementing the changes the organization needed, but there was an unseen dynamic he couldn't quite put his finger on. This dynamic left Jim feeling alone as a leader. When he passionately expressed his desires and plans, he was met with blank stares and a total lack of engagement.

Situational leadership theory says that there are two factors at play with those we lead: competency and motivation. In this case, since competency was not a question, motivation was the factor to zero in on. I requested permission to observe Jim leading his weekly team meeting. It became clear that some cultural norms had been adopted that were undermining the team's ability to reach alignment and move the organization forward. If strategy isn't working, doing a cultural audit is a great way to uncover dynamics that may be undermining success.

I made several observations, but I'll highlight three. First, decision-making power was unclear. Jim said that important decisions would be made collectively as a team. What I observed was Jim asserting his well-formed ideas and shutting down anyone who pushed back. Second, Jim expected each person to have input on agenda items, but he did not provide agenda items ahead of meetings as promised. This put pressure on the team to think on their feet about decisions that required more thought and analysis. As a result,

Jim began to assume they didn't have any good ideas and stopped asking. Third, I noticed a lot of sarcasm. Sarcasm is not necessarily bad if it's couched within the context of safe relationships. In this case, though, sarcasm was used to communicate truth indirectly. These sideways conversations were confusing and chipped away at the sense of safety within the team.

I shared my observations with the group. I then asked each person to give their perspective on each observation and to state their desires for a new cultural norm in that area. Next, I asked the group to collectively come up with new cultural norms for their meetings going forward. Some things they came up with were the following.

1. Jim would present his ideas as rough drafts open to feedback and pushback so the best decisions could be made.
2. The agenda for each meeting would be set at the end of the previous one. Everyone would commit to coming ready to contribute to the discussion and share ideas.
3. Issues were to be dealt with directly, person to person, rather than in meetings in front of the group. The group agreed they needed support in developing better conflict management skills.

These new norms were posted in the room where the team met, and they were revisited at the end of each meeting to ensure adherence. After two months, the new norms became part of the culture.

Jim experienced a gradual shift in getting organizational initiatives and changes pushed forward once the cultural component of the team was addressed. The team began to reach alignment faster, and each member became more engaged and bought in. The leaders were so inspired that they began doing cultural audits organization-wide.

If the strategies you are trying to implement aren't gaining any traction, consider whether increasing your levels of organizational awareness through a cultural audit may be the missing piece!

ACTION STEP

Want to get results like Jim's? Here's what you can do.

Cultural Audit

Ask for a meeting with key influencers in your organization. Ask them how they would describe power relationships, underlying structures, emotional currents, unspoken rules, and informal networks. Consider using the questions below, or hire a consultant to assist you.

Power Relationships and Underlying Structures

- Is there an "in" crowd and an "out" crowd?
- Who has influence?
- What are the attributes of people who get things done?

Emotional Currents of the Group

- Is the group aligned?
- Is there underlying conflict?
- Is there a sense of trust?

Social Considerations

- What are the social networks within the organization?
- Who has influence—in other words, who does key information pass through and who do people listen to?
- What qualities do the influencers possess?
- How do the influencers do things differently?

Day 14

Serving Is the
New Strong

Good leaders must first become good servants.

— ROBERT GREENLEAF

L ike empathy, servant leadership can get a negative
rap, being perceived as the antithesis to strong leadership. I was first exposed to this nontraditional
philosophy in grad school. It's interesting that we often
choose to patronize places based on the quality of service we
receive. Why, then, do we view this quality differently when
leading our teams? This is an interesting question. As leaders, we may find it counterintuitive to focus on serving our
teams when they are working for us and getting paid.
Shouldn't they be serving us? Yes, but the most effective
leaders I have seen also find ways to serve their teams.

One of my favorite stories of servant leadership is about
Jeff Hoffman, multibillionaire and founder of several companies, including the online travel agency Priceline. I attended a
business breakfast where he shared how his team was

working around the clock to meet a deadline. He asked his team if they needed anything, and one of his key developers said he needed someone to pick up his dry cleaning. To everyone's amazement, Hoffman left right then and picked up his dry cleaning. Hoffman knew that to keep good talent, you have to take good care of your team.

Today, we are focusing on increasing our levels of **service orientation**.

WHAT IS SERVICE ORIENTATION?

Service orientation is the ability to anticipate and meet the needs of others. Leaders strong in this skill are concerned with their teams' well-being, supporting their team members' growth and empowerment. They make themselves accessible and are helpful; they provide the necessary resources and remove the obstacles to getting the job done. They also protect their teams, taking care not to overpromise client work to the point of causing burnout. In the context of emotional intelligence at work, cultivating a service orientation means being intentional in seeking ways we can support, assist, and advocate for others.

BENEFITS OF SERVICE ORIENTATION

Leaders with a strong service orientation don't just focus on work getting done; they also focus on meeting the needs of the people performing the work. This activates the natural law of reciprocity that states that when we initiate giving to others, they often feel compelled to give in return. Leaders with a strong service orientation therefore often inspire strong engagement and loyalty from their teams. They also create cultures that are service oriented, influencing the way their teams anticipate and meet the needs of customers and having a direct impact on the bottom line. This also leads to the added benefit of retention of both internal talent and external clients.

SYMPTOMS THAT YOU MAY NEED TO BUILD YOUR SKILL SET IN SERVICE ORIENTATION

- You tend to be more task-focused than people-focused.
- You find yourself consistently burning out your team to meet customer/client demands.
- You rarely ask your team what resources or support they need that could make their work better or easier.

JOHN, DIRECTOR, SOFTWARE DEVELOPMENT COMPANY

My client John had been in the software development industry for many years and had experienced great success. Recently he had been promoted to director and reached out to me for coaching.

He was feeling frustrated with his team because they weren't meeting his expectations and delivering to customers by the deadline. To get a sense of things, I asked him to estimate the percentage of time he spent focusing on his customers versus on his team. He shared that about 80 percent of his attention was focused on his customers and 20 percent on his team.

John's response is very common; it makes sense that leaders would want to focus their time and attention on the revenue-generating parts of the business. It's also important to remember that work gets done *through* the team, so both are important in terms of focus.

John had what I call an old school mentality of leadership. This mentality can include many things, but one of them is the belief that the team is there to serve the leader. While this may be "true," I have seen leaders get a lot more done by putting themselves in a posture of service to their team. When a team's needs are met, they give unparalleled loyalty and performance, which creates a win-win! Being in service to others is a magnetic quality; people want to perform for someone who cares about them.

With this idea in mind, I challenged John to find opportunities to focus more of his time and attention on his team each week. Instead of limiting his interactions with his team members to short transactions that focused on task accomplishment and demands, I suggested he ask his team members what they needed to do their jobs and if there was anything standing in the way that he could help with. The first time he asked those questions, he was met with blank stares until they got used to his approach.

Another opportunity we identified to hone John's skills in service orientation was in meetings.

Typically, John would give the team their tasks and leave little time for questions. When questions were asked, John's frustration that "they should know" was very apparent. I reminded John that his thirty-plus years of experience could add a lot of value to meetings and provide an opportunity to impart his knowledge to others. I encouraged him to think about what he could *give* to his team to help them grow and develop instead of taking a posture of what he could *get* from them. He began asking the team what knowledge they most needed to do their jobs, and he used part of their time in meetings every week to teach and ask questions.

By asking these service-oriented questions and changing

his approach during meetings, he began to glean information that showed him where the performance gaps were so he could address them. He began to feel more connected to his team, and they reciprocated his efforts. He was able to make promises and set deadlines with customers that he could keep based on his knowledge of his team.

As leaders, it's easy to get tunnel vision and focus on the demands of our roles and meeting customer expectations, but serving our teams as if they're our most important customers is one of the secrets to long-lasting success.

ACTION STEP

Want to get results like John's? Here's what you can do.

Service Orientation Quiz

Evaluate the following list. Which statements are true for you? Which areas currently need improvement?

- I have a genuine desire to understand my team's needs (asking questions, listening, and responding).
- I consider the impact the decisions I make has on my team, and I ask for input about these decisions.
- I prioritize my team as much as I prioritize my most important customers/clients.
- I am willing to get my hands dirty with the team versus just telling them what to do.
- My team believes I have their back and will advocate for their needs, concerns, and ideas.
- I am committed to helping my team develop and grow.

For each item you marked as a strength, provide a specific example. For each item you marked as needing improvement, brainstorm an action you can take to begin improving in that area. Use John's story as inspiration for specific areas of focus.

Bonus Action: Get Another Perspective

Your answers to these questions require a certain level of self-awareness. Not sure if your answers are accurate? Ask two people on your team to answer these same questions about you and provide specific examples and suggested action items. Compare your answers with theirs and reflect.

Day 15

Listen for the
Heart Message

[Empathy is] connecting to the emotions that underpin an experience.

— BRENÉ BROWN

Now more than ever, the ability to keep good talent is essential for creating and sustaining an organization that can continue to grow. While there are many factors that influence retention, the relationship that an employee has with their boss is a significant one. According to a study by Businessolver, 96 percent of employees consider it important for their employers to demonstrate empathy, but "92 percent believe empathy remains undervalued" by companies.[1] Stock options, paid vacations, and salary are common considerations for

---

1. *2018 State of Workplace Empathy Executive Summary* (Businessolver, 2018), https://info.businessolver.com/hubfs/empathy-2018/businessolver-empa thy-executive-summary.pdf.

increasing retention, but increasing workplace empathy is surprisingly an often overlooked strategy.

Today, we're again working on increasing our levels of **empathy**.

WHAT IS EMPATHY?

We covered this skill previously, and we are hitting it again here, but from a different angle. As a refresher, empathy is the ability to share and understand the feelings of those around us. In the context of emotional intelligence at work, cultivating empathy means being able to suspend judgment and see a situation from another's perspective. On day 12, we focused on showing empathy by getting curious and asking questions. Today, we're focusing on the ability to see a situation through another person's perspective.

BENEFITS OF EMPATHY

Leaders strong in this skill are able to see things from another's perspective without judgment, even if their perspective differs. They are able to feel "with people" by recognizing others' emotions and acknowledging them. They really listen and seek to understand the members of their teams to ensure they feel seen and heard. As a result, members of their teams are more productive, more likely to share their honest concerns and questions, and more engaged and committed. Even when certain aspects of their jobs are not ideal, people will often stay if they have a positive connection with their leaders.

SYMPTOMS THAT YOU MAY NEED TO BUILD YOUR SKILL SET IN EMPATHY

- Your team experiences a lot of turnover of great talent.
- Your team does not have a culture of healthy vulnerability.
- You aren't sure how to create a connection with others during difficult conversations.

ALLEN, CEO, CONSULTING FIRM

Allen is the CEO of a successful consulting firm and a long-time client of mine. Allen is one of the most fair, thoughtful, and thorough people I know. One of the ways his thoroughness is displayed is in the way he goes about calculating and awarding salary increases and annual bonuses to his executive team. In one particular year, a new team member named Kevin had been added to the team. Kevin was head of people operations and provided tremendous value to the organization. He had saved the company thousands of dollars by tightening up the hiring process, initiating training and development initiatives, and creating a robust intern program. But his role was unique, which made the criteria for evaluating a salary increase and bonus a little unclear. If Allen followed his normal process to set Kevin's increase and bonus, it might not reflect the value Kevin provided—but if Allen were to follow a different process, he would need to convince the partners and the board to do something new.

Allen knew that deviating from the standard process of evaluation would create a new precedent for similar roles in the future, so he stuck with the current process. When Allen met with Kevin about his requested salary increase and bonus, he knew Kevin would be disappointed, as it was significantly less than what he had asked for. Allen didn't provide a detailed explanation, but he acknowledged that it fell short of Kevin's request and that he hoped Kevin didn't quit. Their meeting was short, and Allen didn't give it a second thought.

Allen casually mentioned this conversation to me on one of our coaching calls. I asked him how Kevin felt about the decision, and he said, "Fine, I guess." I had worked with Kevin as well, and based on what I knew about him, I was certain that he would have felt deeply disappointed to not get awarded a salary increase that was in line with industry standards. Allen shared with me that he valued Kevin greatly, but he felt his hands were tied when it came to changing how increases and bonuses were awarded for this new role.

I encouraged Allen to ask Kevin some questions and listen for the heart message. A heart message is something that sounds one way on the surface but means something else when you probe deeper. This is a concept I was introduced to by relationship expert Laura Doyle. Listening for the heart message is another way to practice empathy. To do this, you seek to identify the feeling you can connect with, despite what's being said. Allen asked a series of questions to better understand how Kevin was truly feeling. He also went into more detail to explain the reason behind his decision.

When he did, he learned that Kevin didn't feel valued and was considering looking elsewhere for another job. This is where the opportunity to be empathetic saved the day! Instead of arguing, telling Kevin he shouldn't feel that way, or getting defensive, Allen chose to be empathetic. He let Kevin know that he had never wanted him to question his value, and he went on to explain the extent of the value that he brought. He was also vulnerable and told Kevin that he didn't have the power to change things right away, but he would work on it and hoped that Kevin would stick around to give him that chance. Despite not getting the salary increase and bonus he desired, Kevin felt heard and understood, and a sense of connection and trust was reestablished. Kevin decided to stay.

About nine months later, Allen convinced the other partners and board to reevaluate the processes for awarding salaries and bonuses. He demonstrated the savings in dollars, time, and lack of legal infringements that had been made by having Kevin in place, along with the industry standards for compensation for Kevin's role. He won them over and was able to award not only the desired increase and bonus, but a promotion in title as well. Kevin was elated not just because his desires were met but because he felt valued, seen, and heard throughout the process. If Allen had not acted on the opportunity to show empathy, he likely would have lost an amazing contributor.

ACTION STEP

Want to get results like Allen's? Here's what you can do.

Practice Empathy Hacks

Make a list of some situations and people you could practice more empathy with. Many leaders want to express care for their people, but they aren't sure what to say. To help with this, I developed some empathy hacks, which are things you can say when you don't know what to say. Take a look at the list below and imagine how you might use one of these in the specific situation you just identified.

- "That sounds really hard."
- "I'm in your corner."

- "I am not sure what to say, but I am so glad you told me."
- "What has this been like for you?"
- "I can appreciate how challenging this must be."
- "I hear you."
- "I can relate to that feeling. How can I help?"

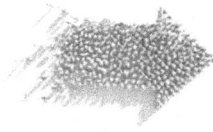

Part IV
Relationship Management

In this section, we continue our focus on our relationships with others. The fourth core competency of leading with emotional intelligence is relationship management. People strong in relationship management have the ability to influence others, are good at developing members of their teams through coaching and mentoring, and address conflict and difficult conversations directly with productive resolutions.

According to a recent survey by the Society for Human Resource Management, "72 percent of employees rank 'respectful treatment of all employees at all levels' as the top factor in job satisfaction."[1] Unresolved conflict can cost companies billions of dollars in lost productivity.[2] In my experience, many companies don't recognize the hard costs associated with conflict such as HR resources, turnover and

---

1. Tamara Lytle, "How to Resolve Workplace Conflicts," Society for Human Resource Management, July 13, 2015, https://www.shrm.org/topics-tools/news/hr-magazine/how-to-resolve-workplace-conflicts.

2. *Workplace Conflict and How Businesses Can Harness It to Thrive* (CPP Global, July 2008).

rehiring costs, and lost productivity as morale decreases. The missing link is often leaders who are unskilled in knowing how to effectively facilitate and productively resolve conflict. These seemingly "soft skills" are connected to hard evidence that affects the bottom line.

In this section, we will cover eleven core skills to help you increase your relationship management:

1. Building trust
2. Powerful influencing skills
3. Interpersonal effectiveness
4. Catalyzing change
5. Building bonds
6. Productive feedback
7. Delegation
8. Coaching
9. Communication
10. Conflict management
11. Inspirational leadership

The quality of the relationships you have with those you lead can transform your experience of leadership from one of duty into one of fulfillment. I have experienced this with every leader I have coached, and you'll get to experience some of their inspiring stories in the pages to follow. Often, all you need to transition from frustration to enjoying leading your team is to develop the right skill set. If you do, you'll see the team you thought could never change become the dream team you always wanted. It all starts with you!

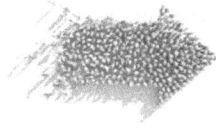

Day 16
Leaders Go First

Courage is rightly esteemed the first of human qualities, because, as has been said, it is the quality which guarantees all others.

— WINSTON CHURCHILL

I was amazed when I heard the story of Roger Bannister, who, in 1954, became the first person to break the four-minute mile. Runners had been seriously chasing this goal since the late 1800s, but until Bannister, it had eluded them. The most powerful part of this story is that just forty-six days after Bannister broke the record, an Australian runner named John Landy set a new record with a time of 3 minutes and 58 seconds, a second faster than Bannister's time. Since then, thousands of runners have also been able to conquer the four-minute barrier.

I love this story because it shows the power of someone going first and demonstrating what's possible. Similarly, I have seen leaders who choose to go first in a challenging area inspire their teams to follow suit.

Today, we are focusing on increasing our skills in **building trust**.

WHAT IS BUILDING TRUST?

Building trust is the ability to secure the confidence of others in our character and abilities. It is the operating system of every relationship. When trust is compromised, the whole system breaks down.

Of all the relationship management skills, this is the one all the others are built upon. In the context of emotional intelligence at work, cultivating trust means acting in ways that not only build trust, but also restore it when it is broken.

BENEFITS OF BUILDING TRUST

Leaders strong in this skill have the full confidence of their teams not because they are perfect, but because they are consistent. They maintain high levels of personal integrity by living out their professed values and following through on their promises and commitments. When they make mistakes, they own them with their teams and make things right. They create a sense of emotional safety, which encourages open, honest, authentic conversations within their teams. When conflicts arise, this strong sense of mutual trust allows difficult conversations to be had without anxiety or fear. Their teams know their leaders have their best interests at heart, and they have confidence that the leaders will respond in ways that are respectful and fair.

SYMPTOMS THAT YOU MAY NEED TO BUILD YOUR SKILL SET IN BUILDING TRUST

- You have experienced high turnover on your team, and you don't know why.
- You have difficulty getting honest and direct feedback from your team. They seem to hold back.
- When mistakes are made, your team tends to blame others rather than taking accountability.

BETH, DIRECTOR, MEDICAL SALES COMPANY

When I met Beth, she was angry and frustrated with her team. She described her team as disengaged in meetings, rarely participating or contributing ideas. She was disappointed with their performance in their respective areas and had recently discovered that several members of her team were seeking employment elsewhere. When she tried to address these things with her team, they shut down.

Beth reached out to me to "fix her team," which is a telltale sign of isolated blame. A team is almost always the product of their leadership, so I anticipated some unrecognized leadership issues would need to be uncovered.

As I have noted in other chapters, the first step is always increasing our self-awareness through feedback. I got Beth's permission to meet individually with each of her senior leaders, and a common theme emerged. There had been an incident a year prior where Beth's actions had completely broken trust with her team. When Beth's leaders had brought the incident up to her, they had felt she was defensive. Ever since then, they had kept her at an arm's length, and she had reacted with anger and frustration. It was a vicious cycle.

After my meetings with the senior leaders, the next step

was to create a safe space for Beth and her team to discuss the incident in hopes of bringing greater levels of understanding and resolve. I served as moderator to ensure that everyone had a voice without interruption and to be the gatekeeper should things get off track. In coaching Beth beforehand, I encouraged her to listen and be open to being accountable for anything she may have done (even unintentionally) that compromised her team's trust in her. One of the best ways to build trust is going first in taking accountability for our reactions and behaviors that have caused others to lose trust in us. People can only trust us to the extent that we own our actions and commit to not repeating them. In this situation, Beth was resistant to this approach and wanted her team's shortcomings to be discussed and apologized for as well. This is completely understandable, but it is almost always ineffective. Building trust takes a leader who is willing to let go of ego and be vulnerable and humble. These qualities create a sense of authenticity in the relationship that elicits trust. It is worth it if you want to create a team that not only trust you but also trusts one another.

While the process was incredibly uncomfortable at times, Beth's team was able to explain the impact her actions had on them. Beth kept her word to go first and apologized for the impact her actions had on the team. That conversation was one of many where we unpacked additional situations that the team felt were unresolved. The dynamic between Beth and her team shifted almost immediately. Beth's humility inspired her team to extend grace to her, and it prompted them to voluntarily own their own reactions and behaviors that were unproductive. It's amazing what a leader who is willing to go first can inspire in the actions of their team. In six months' time, a completely different team culture was created. They had the tools to have unmoderated discussions that were productive.

All members of the senior leadership team decided to stay, proving that the ability to build trust is also an effective retention strategy.

ACTION STEP

Want to get results like Beth's? Here's what you can do.

Accountability Audit

Answer the following questions. Rate yourself on a scale of 1 to 5 for each question (5 being the highest).

1. How would your team rate their ability to trust you as their leader? Consider current levels of engagement, performance, and retention when you answer.
2. How safe does your team feel discussing issues and challenges with you?
3. When you make a mistake, is your tendency to take accountability or blame others?
4. When you want to change something in your team, how willing are you to go first?

Evaluating Your Rating

Total Score: 4–8
Needs improvement. You have the opportunity for intentional focus.

CHAPTER 16

Total Score: 9–15

Good understanding. You have the opportunity for increased mastery.

Total Score: 16–20

Strong mastery. You have the opportunity to continue to level up.

Based on your ratings, what are actions you can take to build greater levels of trust on your team?

Bonus Action: BRAVING Rating

Watch Brené Brown's "The Anatomy of Trust" (https://brenebrown.com/videos/anatomy-trust-video/). She uses the acronym BRAVING to describe seven characteristics of trust. Rate yourself in each of these areas and identify an action you can take in each area to bring your score up.

Day 17

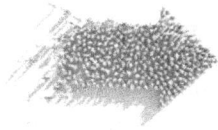

The Power of Influence

You can make more friends in two months by becoming interested in other people than you can in two years by trying to get other people interested in you.

— DALE CARNEGIE

When I got accepted into my choice college, a big price tag came with it. My parents were not able to pay all my college tuition, so I knew I would need to work while going to school. My desire was to be a server at a restaurant so I could earn tips and have a flexible schedule. There was a new restaurant opening, so I applied for a server position, but I was told that because I had no experience, I would have to work my way up. I knew I didn't have time for that, so I got creative. On the day of my interview, I decided to see if I could influence the hiring manager to reconsider by memorizing the menu in detail. That included the pricing of every menu item (complete with upgrades) and the history and values of the company. The manager was so impressed that I got the job without any serving experience!

By knowing what my future employer valued and showing initiative and competence around those skills, I was able to influence a completely different outcome than was originally presented to me. This was a very formative learning experience for me. I learned the importance of focusing on what others value and crafting a message and actions around it. That job not only carried me through my college years, but it taught me an important lesson about influence.

Today, we are focusing on increasing our levels of **powerful influencing skills**.

WHAT ARE POWERFUL INFLUENCING SKILLS?

Like other relationship management skills, powerful influencing skills help us to inspire desired responses and actions in others. In the context of emotional intelligence at work, cultivating powerful influencing skills means becoming someone who people listen to and follow, regardless of title or position. The next two days will focus on different applications of this skill. In this chapter, we'll be focusing on influencing via our communication, while in the next chapter, we'll apply the skill of influence to our peers and teams.

BENEFITS OF POWERFUL INFLUENCING SKILLS

Leaders strong in this skill are good at persuading others. They discover what the people on their teams value, and they create a customized message to win them over. They build consensus within their teams, gaining support for their ideas and inspiring action. They are also masterful storytellers who can engage any audience and leave a lasting impression. Essentially, leadership *is* influence. Without influence, we are leaders in title only.

SYMPTOMS THAT YOU MAY NEED TO BUILD YOUR SKILL SET IN POWERFUL INFLUENCING SKILLS

- You find yourself communicating the same way with everyone instead of customizing your message.
- When presenting your ideas, you notice that they often fall flat or people seem disengaged.
- You have trouble defending your ideas when they are challenged.

FRANK, SENIOR PARTNER, ARCHITECTURAL COMPANY

I had been coaching Frank for a couple months when he asked me to help him prepare for a career-defining presentation. His firm and one other were in the final lineup for a bid to design a new pediatrics wing for a large downtown hospital. Frank had always struggled to communicate his ideas effectively with his team, and he did not want to let them down by blowing the opportunity for a multibillion-dollar job.

The feedback Frank had received regarding his presentation skills was that he lacked the ability to communicate a big-picture vision. He often got caught up in the details and minutiae of how a project would be executed as the client's eyes glazed over. He also tended to focus on highlighting his skills and experience without engaging his audience to hear their ideas and goals for a project. He operated very autonomously and struggled to collaborate. With this feedback as tangible data, I helped him formulate a plan to help him increase his ability to influence and win others over.

The first thing we focused on was establishing a vision for the project. I suggested he meet with the key decision-makers to ask what their desires and outcomes for the project were. I encouraged him to speak only to get clarity and to spend the majority of the time listening.

Second, I suggested he find out exactly who would be in the room on presentation day. Once we had a list, we did extensive research on each attendee to determine their values and what information would be most relevant to them so that we could determine what to include. Third, I set him up to interview a friend of mine who had a child who spent the majority of her childhood in hospitals being treated for cancer. Frank learned how important small details of design were to creating a comforting and family-friendly environment. Finally, we studied the other firm in the running and learned that they were equally competent, so we had to find our edge. Given that the hospital project would take seven years, our competitive edge became showcasing that Frank's team would be the most enjoyable and desirable to work with.

Frank and I practiced the presentation to ensure it fell well within the designated time frame and let each of his team members shine in their respective roles. The communication was customized to address the values and areas of interest each attendee and decision-maker had expressed. Frank adjusted his communication to only include the high-level concepts of design and did not get into the weeds unless asked a question. After the presentation, Frank said that the response was positive and everyone was engaged from start to finish.

Learning about the values of your audience and adjusting your message to speak to those values is key for having effective influence and leaving a lasting impression. Two weeks later, we received the great news that Frank's team had won the bid. When asked about the deciding factor for choosing Frank's firm over the other, the hospital director said he thought both firms were equally competent, but he would rather work with Frank's team. He felt they best understood the vision and were most tuned in with the stakeholders' desires and outcomes for the project.

The first step in increasing powerful influencing skills, both within your team and with clients, is to understand what those you are trying to influence value and tailor your communication to those values.

ACTION STEP

Want to get results like Frank's? Here's what you can do.

Influence Presentation

Identify a decision or initiative where you need the support of others to be successful.

You might practice with something that only needs the support of one or two other people.

Then go through these steps.

Do you have a clear vision for the outcome of the initiative? If not, get clear about the objective and benefit.

Next, make a list of who you want to influence, what they value, and what concerns they may have. If you are not sure, seek out that information and create a more customized communication strategy. Leave space for interactions and questions. Practice your presentation with a colleague first to get initial feedback. Make any necessary changes and present your initiative to your team or client.

Reflect on how your presentation was received. Were people engaged? Get feedback and continue to hone your influence.

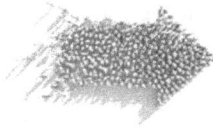

Day 18
Building Relational Equity

Talented people are attracted to those who care about them.

— ADAM GRANT

The best-selling book *How to Win Friends and Influence People* by Dale Carnegie is a timeless classic whose principles continue to provide today's leaders with practical tools for success. Carnegie's fundamental principles focus on how to handle people well so that they like you and are willing to be influenced by you. Since the very essence of leadership is the ability to influence others, it makes sense that his book has remained relevant today. Some leaders will say they are not in leadership to be liked. While we can't please everyone, it's a lot easier to lead people who have a positive affinity toward you, who are open to being influenced by you, and who give you their best efforts not because of your position but because they genuinely want to. These skills may seem like common sense to some, but they are completely unrecognized areas of struggle for others, so it's worth a second chapter to emphasize them again.

Today, we're again working on increasing our levels of **powerful influencing skills**.

WHAT ARE POWERFUL INFLUENCING SKILLS?

We are hitting this one again because influence is such a vital component of leadership. Powerful influencing skills help us to inspire desired actions and responses in others. They make us someone who people listen to and follow regardless of title or position. Yesterday, we focused on the communication aspect of powerful influencing skills, and today, we're applying the skill of influence to our peers and teams.

BENEFITS OF POWERFUL INFLUENCING SKILLS

Leaders strong in this skill know how to build rapport with people. They learn what makes each person tick, and they adjust their approach accordingly. They discern when to be assertive, when to make suggestions, and when to ask questions. They listen and appeal to what others value to persuade and influence. As a result, people are interested in their ideas because they have inspired true commitment versus compliance.

SYMPTOMS THAT YOU MAY NEED TO BUILD YOUR SKILL SET IN POWERFUL INFLUENCING SKILLS

- You aren't sure what motivates those you are seeking to influence.
- You rely on the authority of your title instead of using influence to get things done.

- You tend to focus more on getting work done than on building relationships with others.

SAM, CREATIVE DIRECTOR, ENTERTAINMENT INDUSTRY

My client Sam is a brilliant creative in the entertainment industry. While he is wildly successful in his work, he experiences a lot of challenges in his relationships with his peers. When Sam reached out to me for coaching, his company had just landed its biggest project to date, and to complete the project, he would be working in close partnership with a peer he had a strained relationship with. He knew his relationship with that peer needed to improve, but he wasn't sure where to start.

Thriving relationships have a good amount of relational equity built into them. Relationships are like bank accounts —we are either making deposits or withdrawals in our everyday interactions. Sam had made a lot of withdrawals that really grated on the peer he'd be working with, so we came up with a plan to build relational equity. When you have relational equity, influence is easier and mistakes are met with more grace.

I asked Sam if he could answer a couple questions about his peer:

- What was important to her in working together?
- What stressed her out?
- What were her goals/vision for the work?

Sam admitted he couldn't answer these questions with certainty. This is common! Often, we can become so focused on our own work that we don't seek to understand others. As a first step, I suggested that Sam initiate a lunch with his peer, communicating his desire to get on the same page so the project could be successful. During the lunch, he asked her the three questions, and he received great insight into the things that could make or break their relationship. I also suggested that he ask her for feedback as to what he could do to best support her in making the project successful. She was surprised by this and softened to his willingness to improve their relationship. He received the feedback without getting defensive or making excuses, whether he agreed with the feedback or not.

Once Sam had clarity on what he could do to improve the relationship, we came up with some action items. I also suggested he meet with his peer on a regular basis outside of their project meetings to check in to ensure he was on track with his efforts.

There was also feedback he wanted to share, but I suggested he hold off until he had enough relational equity to do so. Months later, he was able to share some of his desires and needs for the working relationship, and his peer was very receptive. Mistakes were still made from time to time, but Sam and his peer had grace for one another when those times happened.

Our results are always dependent upon the quality of our relationships. Sam and his peer not only delivered outstanding results in their project, but they enjoyed their working relationship along the way—a true win-win!

ACTION STEP

Want to get results like Sam's? Here's what you can do.

Relational Equity Exercise

1. Choose someone who you would like to have a better rela-

tionship and greater influence with. Take ten to fifteen minutes to answer these questions on your own:

- What is important to them in working together?
- What are their stressors/triggers?
- What is their vision/goal?

2. Set up a short meeting with the person you chose and ask them the same questions.

3. Evaluate: How do your answers compare? What new insights did you gain? What are a couple of new actions you can take to increase your relational equity with this person?

4. Take action and note any positive changes in the relationship.

Day 19
Make a
Connection

Seek first to understand, then to be understood.

— STEPHEN COVEY

I was a Navy brat and grew up all over the US, moving states every couple of years. Despite not leaving the country, I got a rich cultural experience within all the diverse subcultures in each place. I grew up with people from Cuba, Latin America, India, the Philippines, Mexico, Japan, and various parts of the UK and Europe. My playmates exposed me to new foods, games, traditions, and experiences. Although it was challenging to move around so much, I didn't realize until adulthood how enriching those experiences were in equipping me to relate to people different from myself.

The way that I saw this really play out was when I went abroad to do relief work. I led a team of people who had never been out of the country before. As a leader, I was able to effortlessly connect with people of all ages and backgrounds and find common ground quickly. Some of my team-mates, though, felt really challenged throughout the experience. They really struggled to adjust to a new culture; they wanted to go home; the food was too spicy. They had a hard time making connections with people different from them. One of the greatest pitfalls that leaders can fall into is only being able to relate to people just like them. This can become a major cognitive bias that can lead to playing favorites and can create an obstacle to realizing your team's full potential.

Today, we are focusing on increasing our levels of **interpersonal effectiveness**.

WHAT IS INTERPERSONAL EFFECTIVENESS?

Like other relationship management skills, interpersonal effectiveness refers to the people skills needed to build effective and rewarding relationships with others. In the context of emotional intelligence at work, cultivating interpersonal effectiveness means building a skill set that allows us to connect and get along with all different types of people, using skills like being attuned to others, communicating effectively, and putting others at ease.

BENEFITS OF INTERPERSONAL EFFECTIVENESS

Leaders strong in this skill have the ability to build rapport and connection with everyone on their teams, even those very different from themselves. They take a genuine interest in each individual team member, are good listeners, and adjust their communication approach based on their read on people. When there is tension within their teams, they know how to defuse it and restore rapport. They are especially good at finding common ground and winning over their critics.

Leaders strong in interpersonal effectiveness create teams that are genuinely aligned and committed, both to the leaders themselves and to other team members.

SYMPTOMS THAT YOU MAY NEED TO BUILD YOUR SKILL SET IN INTERPERSONAL EFFECTIVENESS

- You find it difficult to connect or find common ground with people on your team who are different from you.
- When there is a conflict or misunderstanding with someone on your team, you find it difficult to restore rapport.
- Instead of fully listening, you often interject with your opinions and solutions.

REBECCA, HUMAN RESOURCES MANAGER, CITY GOVERNMENT

Rebecca is a gifted HR practitioner who had quickly moved up the ranks because of her skillful and thorough approach to handling a variety of complex situations for the city.

Despite her past successes, she showed up to our first coaching session with a great deal of reserve and apprehension. She shared with me that she had recently been asked to oversee the city's DEI committee as an interim director until a new hire was made. What made this role intimidating for her was leading a group of people of color as a Caucasian woman. She believed in the mission of the role, but she was worried about how she would be received. An additional challenge Rebecca faced was conducting all team meetings over Zoom because of the COVID lockdown.

As a person who grew up in diverse environments my

112

entire life, I consider having relationships with people very different from myself to be a strong personal value. I was excited about helping Rebecca create meaningful connections and earn the trust of her team.

Rebecca described the first couple of meetings as painful as she attempted to go through the agenda she created, only to be met with blank stares and a lack of response when questions were asked. Some participants didn't turn their cameras on, making any sort of connection even more challenging.

I encouraged Rebecca to view this as a welcomed challenge to hone her skills in interpersonal effectiveness. The first thing that I suggested was to create individual relationships with each person on the team by setting up one-on-ones, either virtually or in person over coffee. The goal for these meetings was for Rebecca to get to know each person and to discover why they had joined the committee, what they hoped to see accomplished, and what part on the team they hoped to play to bring initiatives forward. Focusing on serving the needs of those you lead versus trying to prove your leadership capabilities almost always opens a door to connection. The majority of the one-on-ones went well, and Rebecca got some valuable information from the group.

Next, we identified the most engaged members of the group and asked those members to help collaborate on the agenda for each week's meeting. Rebecca asked them to facilitate discussion with the group around the topics they were most passionate about. In just one month's time, the group was notably more engaged and receptive to Rebecca's leadership.

Once we had a foundation of relationships, we built on that. I suggested that Rebecca follow up with at least one person after each week's meeting to provide genuine appreciation for what they had contributed to the discussion and to ask how she could support them in their role. For the few members who were still keeping Rebecca at arm's length, this provided another opportunity to build rapport.

After a couple months of working with the DEI committee, Rebecca was asked by the city to present their initiatives for the coming year. We both agreed that the presentation should be facilitated by members of the committee. Rebecca provided the introduction and close, but she let her team take the lead with communicating the various initiatives they had ownership of.

At the end of her six-month interim, Rebecca had completely bonded with her team. When a new director was hired, her team threw an appreciation lunch and told her they wished she was continuing in the role. This is the power of interpersonal effectiveness, which can help bridge seemingly impossible divides. And, as a result of her effectiveness, Rebecca was promoted to a position that included overseeing the new DEI director. Rebecca and her team were excited to keep their connection going, and they continue to do great work together!

ACTION STEP

Want to get results like Rebecca's? Here's what you can do.
(Choose one or both of the following exercises.)

On Common Ground Individual Exercise

Identify the person on your team who is the most different from you, someone you do not have a strong natural connection with, or both. Invite the person you choose out to lunch with the intention of getting to know them better and discovering some things you have in common. This will involve asking them questions about themselves and making connections about things you value (for example, maybe you both have a similar hobby, like the same sports team, or grew up in the same area).

On Common Ground Group Exercise

At the start of your next team meeting, ask each team member to pair up with someone they don't know well. Give each pair ten minutes to make a list of as many things they have in common as possible. Make it a competition! When the time is up, have each group share their list with the group. Typically, this leads to a lot of laughter and fun discoveries about what people have in common despite their apparent differences. It creates a sense of bonding and helps your team develop interpersonal effectiveness by asking good questions.

Day 20
Slower Is Faster

Every minute you spend in planning saves 10 minutes in execution; this gives you a 1,000 percent return on energy.

— BRIAN TRACY

"Slower is faster" is a concept I was introduced to throughout my graduate work and first internal consulting job. In a fast-paced world, the philosophy of "slower is faster" can seem counterintuitive, but it depends what you are applying it to. It's a good idea when you are choosing a life partner and making other life-altering decisions, for example. Another interesting application is sports—kayakers are told to only apply 85 percent of their effort to keep the boat consistently level to efficiently make it to their destination, and runners are taught the importance of training with some slow runs to build long-term endurance. In working with leaders to develop strategies for change and implementing new initiatives, I have learned the importance of slowing down to do the important work needed to get engagement when things get rolled out. You either spend the time on the front end (in other words, go slow) or, later, you have to spend time on the back end cleaning up unnecessary missteps.

Today, we are focusing on increasing our skills in **catalyzing change**.

WHAT IS CATALYZING CHANGE?

Catalyzing change is the ability to initiate, manage, and lead necessary change. In the context of emotional intelligence at work, catalyzing change means being someone who challenges the status quo and can influence others toward new beliefs and actions. Leading change is one of the key abilities that distinguishes a leader. Leaders recognize when a change is needed and know how to effectively enlist their teams to get buy-in. They create an effective strategy for change that includes a compelling reason why the change is needed, the benefits of the change, and a clear process for how the change will be implemented. They take the time to address their teams' concerns and know how to engage those resistant to change. They are visionaries who want to remain innovative and constantly improve things.

BENEFITS OF CATALYZING CHANGE

One of the main differences between managers and leaders is their approach to change. Leaders have the ability to catalyze change. Leaders are the change-makers, while managers manage those changes through process implementation. Catalyzing change is one of the most important functions of a leader—and one of the most challenging.

SYMPTOMS THAT YOU MAY NEED TO BUILD YOUR SKILL SET IN CATALYZING CHANGE

- You tend to implement changes on the fly without a clear strategy.
- You find it difficult to convince your team that changes are necessary.
- You tend to be more reactive to change versus proactive in pursuing necessary change.

MIKE, CEO, ENGINEERING FIRM

My client Mike enlisted me to help him lead one of the most important changes in his company's history. Mike had started a successful engineering firm and run it for 30 years. In preparation for retirement, he reached out to me to help him create a succession plan that would include selecting a new CEO who the company would embrace. He had his own thoughts about who might be the best choice, and he was tempted to just put that person in place and go forward. Fortunately, he had learned from experience that implementing change without a strategy and process can prove to be disastrous, and he wanted to do things differently this time.

The first thing Mike and I did was identify the key leaders who were the most influential in the company and would be most affected by the change. We decided to focus on leadership at the executive and senior levels. For a change of this magnitude, getting good information by soliciting feedback was key. Here is where the saying "slower is faster" applies. If the right information can be gathered and the work can be done on the front end, the actual implementation becomes a smoother process. In this case, I recommended that we conduct confidential interviews with each leader to get honest feedback around five core questions:

1. Where is the company already strong?
2. Where do you see the company in five years, when it's operating at its full potential?
3. What characteristics does a leader need to realize this vision?
4. Who, internally or externally, would you recommend for the position?
5. What do you think needs to be included in this process to implement this change successfully?

The interviews took several months to complete, but the information proved to be invaluable. It allowed us to mitigate potential issues and discover what people wanted in their next leader. As a result, we ended up getting 100 percent buy-in, and the transition to the new CEO was smooth and successful! When it comes to catalyzing change successfully, I have learned that taking the time to create a strategy and process can make all the difference in ensuring that a change is embraced and sustained over the long term. Three years later, the new CEO continues to make great strides within his role and still has the full support of his team!

ACTION STEP

Want to get results like Mike's? Here's what you can do.

Plan a Change Strategy

Identify a change that you want to implement well and begin to make a plan to implement that change.

My favorite framework for change is Kotter's change

model. Here are his eight steps for creating a clear change strategy:

1. Create a sense of urgency.
2. Build a guiding coalition.
3. Form a strategic vision and initiatives.
4. Enlist a volunteer army.
5. Enable action by removing barriers.
6. Generate short-term wins.
7. Sustain acceleration.
8. Institute change.[1]

Let's dive deeper into what each of these steps entails.

1. Create a sense of urgency.

Determine your why, the benefits, and the loss of opportunity that would come with not making the change.

2. Build a guiding coalition.

Connect with those who have influence and are going to be most affected by the change; get their feedback.

3. Form a strategic vision and initiatives.

Create a clear vision of the future the change is going to create.

---

1. *8 Steps to Accelerate Change in Your Organization* (Kotter, 2018).

4. Enlist a volunteer army.

Engage those from your guiding coalition to help promote and implement the change.

5. Enable action by removing barriers.

Support the change by ensuring that processes and resources support the change.

6. Generate short-term wins.

Don't wait until the change is complete; celebrate and reward milestones along the way

7. Sustain acceleration.

Evaluate the effectiveness of the change; get feedback and make tweaks where needed.

8. Institute change.

Communicate connections between the changes and results. Ensure leaders are consistently implementing change across teams and that the organization's systems and structures can sustain the change.

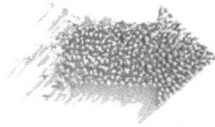

Day 21
Making Relational Pit Stops

When leaders throughout an organization take an active, genuine interest in the people they manage, when they invest real time to understand employees at a fundamental level, they create a climate for greater morale, loyalty, and, yes, growth.

— PATRICK LENCIONI

One of my favorite TV shows years ago was *Undercover Boss*. If you haven't seen it, the basic premise involves the president or CEO of a struggling company disguising themself and working on their business's front lines to gain the insights they need to make their company successful again. It's comical to watch a CEO flounder with basic tasks, and it's inspiring to see them value and build relationships with people at all levels of their organizations. The distance between the proverbial ivory tower and the front lines is a common enough occurrence for there to be a show about it. The show's message speaks to the importance of leaders taking the time to listen to their key people, solicit their input on solving problems, and support their career aspirations. Building these bonds results in long-time problems being solved quickly, staff being valued and retained, and the leader having a better pulse on what's happening within their organization.

Today, we are focusing on increasing our skills in **building bonds**.

WHAT IS BUILDING BONDS?

Building bonds is the ability to create and maintain relationships with all different types of people across a broad network. In the context of emotional intelligence at work, cultivating the skill of building bonds means maintaining an ongoing connection with those on our teams and those we work with in other departments, from the janitor to the VP. It's not just reaching out when we need something. Leaders strong in this skill are intentional about making themselves approachable and accessible.

BENEFITS OF BUILDING BONDS

Leaders who build bonds find that they are able to get things done more quickly and easily. Because of their relationships with people throughout their organizations, their requests are often prioritized and expedited, allowing them to break through the red tape. Information crucial to making informed decisions is shared organically with them through regular interactions versus irregular formal meetings. Problems are identified earlier and solved more quickly, as these leaders get input and feedback from those closest to the work. Key people are also retained, as their feedback is valued and implemented. Overall, these leaders have a great pulse on what is happening in real time throughout all levels of their organizations.

SYMPTOMS THAT YOU MAY NEED TO BUILD YOUR SKILL SET IN BUILDING BONDS

- You don't have relationships with people at all levels of your organization.
- You notice that others are not showing a sense of urgency in helping you get things done.
- You don't see a need to connect with people in other departments unless you need something.

GEORGE, CEO, MANUFACTURING COMPANY

One of my most memorable clients is George. As the CEO for a manufacturing company, he grew up under more traditional philosophies on management that included a focus on tasks and results. When he attended one of my Leading with Emotional Intelligence workshops, his eyes were opened to the difference between management and leadership. While he had the science of management down, the art of leadership was something that intrigued him. He began to wonder whether the business was hitting a ceiling because of a limited focus that didn't include building relationships and developing the people in key roles throughout the organization. He immediately signed up for my three courses on leading with emotional intelligence and decided to conduct an experiment to see if deploying these relationship-building skills would make a difference. He also signed up for coaching to reinforce what he was learning in the courses.

When I met George, he was experiencing three identifiable challenges: (1) he had inherited a senior staff of a family-run business who were not passionate about or gifted in their roles, (2) turnover had started to increase across various key roles, and (3) despite having a steady stream of business coming in, the company was hitting a profit ceiling. George speculated about why those challenges were happening, but he wasn't certain. I asked him a series of questions to prompt him to describe the quality of the relationships he had with the people associated with each of his challenges. His answers revealed that these key relationships were more transactional than relational. I encouraged him to focus on building bonds in these relationships. For the next month, George had one-on-one meetings with each member of the senior leadership team to learn more about them, their roles, and their career aspirations. He also began gathering his key leaders to share their thoughts on what was working and what they saw as development opportunities for the company. Finally, he decided to create some margin in his schedule to make space for intentional conversations with the guys on the floor who were running the machines every day. Each day, he spoke with a different guy on the floor on his way to and from meetings.

By the end of the month, George had not only learned information that revealed why the company was struggling, he had built relationships with people who wanted to help solve the challenges with him. Over the course of the several months that followed, George was able to reposition and release some of the senior staff, address the core reasons for retention issues, and learn what processes and limitations with the current equipment were limiting growth from the frontline workers. The ability to build bonds always results in mutually beneficial outcomes. Since our work together, leading with emotional intelligence is now second nature to George. Not only has his business become more profitable, but the quality of his leadership has become richer.

ACTION STEP

Want to get results like George's? Here's what you can do.

Building Bonds Exercise

Identify a current challenge you are having. Answer the following questions:

- Who are the key people involved in the challenge?
- How would you describe the quality of the relationships you have with each of them?
- Are these relationships nurtured and maintained on an ongoing basis or only when you need something?
- Consider George's story as an example. How can you strengthen your skills in building bonds?
- What are some ways you can serve and help others succeed to create mutually beneficial relationships?

Once you have answered these questions, schedule time with key people across departments and roles. Find ways to maintain ongoing touchpoints throughout the year.

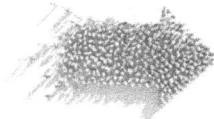

Day 22
The 8-Letter
F-Word

Feedback is the breakfast of champions.

— KEN BLANCHARD

As leaders, one of the most important aspects of our role is creating a strong sense of teamwork and collaboration. In his book *The Five Dysfunctions of a Team*, Patrick Lencioni identifies five barriers that undermine effective teams: (1) absence of trust, (2) fear of conflict, (3) lack of commitment, (4) avoidance of accountability, and (5) inattention to results.[1] In my experience, a golden thread that connects these dysfunctions is a culture lacking in the ability to give productive feedback. Feedback allows honest and helpful insights to be exchanged in a way that brings necessary change and deepens relationships. Unfortunately, feedback has become an eight-letter F-word in many organi-

---

1. Patrick Lencioni, *The Five Dysfunctions of a Team: A Leadership Fable* (Jossey-Bass, 2002), 188.

zations. People avoid giving it, and they brace themselves when receiving it. Few of us received training or good role modeling when it comes to giving and receiving feedback. I find leaders are either direct (and hurtful) or avoidant (and confusing). It doesn't have to be that way! The ability to give productive feedback is a learned skill and well worth the effort. When it is done well, it allows us to create a sense of vulnerability that builds trust, reduces the fear of conflict, helps us make aligned decisions that garner commitment, and lays the groundwork for holding one another accountable for results.

Today, we are focusing on increasing our skills in **productive feedback**.

WHAT IS PRODUCTIVE FEEDBACK?

Productive feedback is the clear, constructive information and guidance that we give to others to support their growth. Feedback can be received top-down, bottom-up, or peer to peer. In the context of emotional intelligence at work, a leader who excels at giving productive feedback is someone who is willing to speak up when things aren't working and give input in a way that is both truthful and respectful. Leaders strong in this skill provide ongoing feedback for individuals on their teams so they always know where they stand. They avoid unhealthy triangulation by encouraging team members to address conflicts directly with one another. They also cultivate a culture within their teams where conflicts are addressed and brought to resolution instead of avoided.

BENEFITS OF PRODUCTIVE FEEDBACK

Leaders who give productive feedback—free of blame or shame and focused on helping others grow—model and encourage a skill set for their teams and organizations to do the same.

Feedback provides an opportunity for expectations to be clarified, creating greater levels of commitment and accountability within the team. Fears around conflict also disappear, as team members are confident problems will be resolved in a way that feels safe. Trust is built because interactions are authentic and transparent. As a result, work gets done better and faster and teams collaborate instead of working against each other. Giving productive feedback is also an effective retention strategy, as people have confidence that their leader is invested and committed to their growth and career development.

SYMPTOMS THAT YOU MAY NEED TO BUILD YOUR SKILL SET IN PRODUCTIVE FEEDBACK

- You wait until formal performance reviews to give feedback.
- Your team tends to avoid conflict and having difficult conversations.
- Your team is inconsistent in being accountable and getting work done.

HAZEL, CEO, PHYSICAL THERAPY CLINIC

Hazel is the founder and CEO of a thriving physical therapy and wellness practice. Her clinic is known for being able to address complex cases with high rates of success. When

Hazel reached out to me for coaching, she wanted to level up her skills in creating greater teamwork and collaboration within her team. Her areas of struggle were responding to conflict, managing different personalities, providing clear expectations, holding people accountable, and providing effective feedback. All these areas are important skills for leaders, but getting the feedback piece right would have a direct impact on all the other areas.

As mentioned earlier, I find leaders can either be direct (and hurtful) or avoidant (and confusing) with their feedback. Hazel was avoidant, but she wanted to become skilled and help her team become skilled with one another. I took Hazel through a clarifying exercise, asking her to identify the purpose of feedback and what she wanted the ground rules to be when giving feedback. I then asked her to make a commitment to be the gatekeeper of those ground rules with her team.

Hazel expressed her fear that feedback could come across as punitive because it tended toward the negative, even if a couple pieces of positive feedback were mixed in. Many leaders feel this way and therefore dread performance reviews and giving ongoing feedback. I believe the purpose of feedback is to give someone the information they need to succeed and fulfill their potential. Rather than calling people *out*, feedback can be a mechanism for calling people *up*. This posture immediately reframes how feedback is given.

Next, Hazel and I collaborated on some ground rules for giving feedback within her team:

1. The purpose of feedback is to help others grow and learn; avoid giving feedback when you are angry.
2. Prepare thoughtful feedback ahead of time; feedback should not be an off-the-cuff complaint session.

3. Do not speak on behalf of others; speak from your own experience.
4. Be direct *and* kind; speak the truth in love.
5. Ask for the other person's perspective on the feedback you give; you could be missing information that causes you to draw incorrect conclusions.

When giving positive feedback, a great question to ask yourself is, What are they already doing that I want to encourage them to continue? When giving developmental feedback, a great question to ask yourself is, What could they do more of to succeed? These questions ensure you are offering balanced feedback. The second question in particular forces you to state what you desire instead of what you want someone to stop (for example, "I would love to see you share more ideas in meetings—I think you have a lot of value to offer."). After our collaboration, Hazel shared the clarified purpose and ground rules around feedback. She was met with relief and excitement. People were longing for direction in how to give feedback well while maintaining a sense of safety and trust within the team.

Hazel did a whole-team feedback session to practice and saw great results! Things were said that needed to be said, and they were said in the right spirit. People felt their fellow team members were "for them" and were grateful for clear information about how to succeed. Once they got practice with one another, they gained confidence in their ability to do the same with their teams. No longer is *feedback* a word that makes Hazel and her team cringe; it's a welcomed experience to gain insight into winning in their roles.

ACTION STEP

Want to get results like Hazel's? Here's what you can do.

Assess Whether You're Ready to Give Feedback

Complete Brené Brown's Engaged Feedback Checklist (https://brenebrown.com/wp-content/uploads/2021/09/ DaringFeedbackChecklist_092921-Dare-to-Lead.pdf). This will help you determine if you are in the right posture and mindset to be giving feedback.

Create Feedback Ground Rules

Create your own list of do's and don'ts when giving feedback. This is a great activity to collaborate with your team on. Practice your new ground rules with your team. As the leader, be the gentle gatekeeper of the new rules as people learn a new way of doing things.

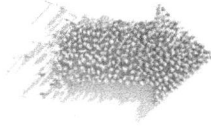

Day 23
Let It Go

The best executive is the one who has sense enough to pick good men to do what he wants done, and self-restraint to keep from meddling with them while they do it.

— THEODORE ROOSEVELT

A popular song in 2013 was the song "Let it Go" from the Disney movie *Frozen*. The song's popularity transcended age groups and was embraced by young and old alike across the world. Besides winning numerous awards, the song became one of the most globally recorded Disney songs, with versions sung in twenty-five languages. Why the appeal? I believe the song taps into every human's desire for autonomy and freedom. While leaders have an extraordinary drive for achievement, there's also an equal need to be able to share the burden of responsibility with others they trust. This is an essential component to creating sustainable achievement.

Today, we are focusing on increasing our levels of **delegation**.

WHAT IS DELEGATION?

Delegation is a key relationship management skill that involves a process of entrusting tasks, decisions, and other responsibilities to other qualified people. In the context of emotional intelligence at work, cultivating skills in delegation means sharing the work and credit with others instead of maintaining a tight grip of control and micromanaging.

BENEFITS OF DELEGATION

Leaders strong in this skill have high levels of self-awareness and know their own capacities and limits. They don't try to do everything themselves—instead, they assign tasks to their teams to create efficient and sustainable workflows. They know the strengths and interests of their teams and assign work accordingly. They stay out of the weeds so that they can create the most value in strategically leading the efforts of their teams. As a result, leaders who are strong in delegation have teams that are competent, empowered, and trusted. Decisions are not bottlenecked, and leaders can go on vacation knowing their teams can handle things.

SYMPTOMS THAT YOU MAY NEED TO BUILD YOUR SKILL SET IN DELEGATION

- You find yourself often in the weeds instead of focusing on higher-level work where you can offer the most value.

- You have a hard time trusting others enough to hand over important tasks or decisions.
- You have a tendency to micromanage when you delegate work to others.

BLANCA, CFO, ACCOUNTING FIRM

When I met Blanca, she was experiencing a challenge every leader has as they continue to expand in their role and responsibilities: the challenge of letting go through delegation! Delegation is one of those leadership functions that has to be evaluated continuously for two primary reasons: (1) to ensure you are focusing on the functions of your role with the highest importance for your skill set, and (2) to ensure you are providing your team with continuous development opportunities.

Blanca was a high-performing CFO with an impeccable track record of excellence in keeping her company's financials organized and in the black. As the company began to grow, she became overwhelmed with the demands of her expanding role; she was spending her evenings and weekends working just to keep up.

When we began coaching together, Blanca expressed that her greatest desire was to continue to deliver exceptional results and continuously improve systems and processes that could support sustainable growth. We started with making a list of the most important functions of her role that *could not* be delegated and a list of those tasks that *could* be delegated with some training. This highlighted the need for a new hire. We then created updated job descriptions for each member of her team with additional delegated responsibilities that matched their skill set. We confirmed with the team that the additional responsibilities matched their current capacities, skill sets, and desires for career development. We made any adjustments where needed.

After hiring an additional member for the team, we created two important systems: (1) ongoing training and (2) communication about task and project progress and completion. Many leaders I work with think that they do not have the time to train, but it saves a tremendous amount of time in the long run when the tasks are delegated and are now being done by capable team members. In Blanca's case, we mapped out a three-month schedule of slowly releasing tasks over time and reserving a small block of time each week for training. I also suggested that Blanca collaborate with her team to set up a task and project tracking system they could all access. Once the system was established, Blanca could check on the status of projects and tasks the team was working on at any time. I also helped her establish a weekly check-in time with her team and suggested she establish a good cadence of one-on-ones with her key team members. As a rule of thumb, I suggest to leaders that they prioritize the members on their teams who need the most support and guidance first and that they set a cadence they can follow through on.

When you start to get intentional about delegation, it can feel like more work for a while before its intended purpose is realized; this is normal. Between the three- and six-month mark, you should start to notice a difference in your workload, the trust you have in your team, and your team's growth. An added bonus is that you can go on vacation and take time off, knowing your team can handle things well while you are away! This was the true test for Blanca. For the first time in many years, she took time off and could fully unplug and enjoy her time away knowing she had created a fully capable team. In the months that followed, Blanca helped support her company with new levels of growth because she now had the time and space to focus on overall organizational development. It was a win all around!

ACTION STEP

Want to get results like Blanca's? Here's what you can do.

Complete a Delegation Exercise

(Choose one or both of the following options.)

Quick Fix

Identify one thing that could be delegated and make a concrete plan to delegate it.

Long Term

List the responsibilities in your role that are essential for you to maintain based on your experience and skill set and the ones you could delegate to others with some training. Assign the delegated responsibilities to your various team members based on current capacities, skill sets, and desired career-development goals. Invite your team to weigh in on some of these decisions to inspire buy-in. Evaluate if any new hires are needed and then draw up new job descriptions for each role. Create an incremental training schedule and collaborate with your team to create a system for communication for task and project tracking everyone can access. Evaluate progress and make any necessary adjustments. As a reward for letting go and delegating, plan a vacation to celebrate your team being empowered to run things without you!

Day 24
The Coaching Advantage

I absolutely believe that people, unless coached, never reach
their maximum potential.

— BOB NARDELLI

E ven though I'm not a sports fan, I have an affinity
for coaches/leaders of sports teams. One of my
favorite coaches is John Wooden, who coached the
UCLA Bruins to win ten national championships. In addition
to his team's accomplishments, Wooden won many personal
awards, including winning national coach of the year seven
times. He was also named coach of the century by ESPN.

His career success demonstrates the important link between
a leader's coaching skills and the level of success a team can
achieve. Wooden had a unique approach in that he didn't focus
as much on the scoreboard as he did on helping everyone on the
team be the best they could be. As a result, the scoreboard took
care of itself. As leaders, it's easy to focus solely on results and

the bottom line. The majority of the leaders I work with really struggle with the coaching aspect of their roles. The good news is that you do not need to be a professional coach to create a winning team; you just need the right tools.

Today, we are focusing on increasing our skills in **coaching**.

WHAT IS COACHING?

Coaching is a series of one-on-one conversations focused on improving skills, knowledge, and performance. In the context of emotional intelligence at work, cultivating the skill of coaching means being intentional about supporting the growth and development of others less experienced than us. Leaders strong in this skill meet with team members regularly to set goals and give ongoing guidance and feedback. Coaches know their mentees' career aspirations and provide a clear path for achievement. They also know how to ask good questions versus just giving answers. Like many other leadership skills, coaching is not often taught, and it can be challenging for leaders who have never experienced coaching themselves.

BENEFITS OF COACHING

Leaders who are committed to ongoing coaching and mentoring experience several benefits: accelerated growth and performance of their teams, development of independent problem solvers, greater retention and loyalty, and a larger bench of future leaders.

Having been a coach since 2012 and having received coaching myself throughout the years, I can attest to the significant difference coaching makes in all these areas.

CHAPTER 24

SYMPTOMS THAT YOU MAY NEED TO BUILD YOUR SKILL SET IN COACHING

- You don't have regular one-on-ones with your key team members.
- You rely solely upon companywide trainings to develop your team.
- You don't have a good understanding of your team members' career aspirations.

SHAWN, PRESIDENT, RECRUITING AGENCY

Shawn was one of my consulting clients when he reached out for me to help him create a leadership development program for his organization that included a course on coaching for his leaders. At the time, his industry was experiencing a huge influx of work just as his organization was seeing an increase in turnover from some of his most experienced people. While there were a couple of reasons identified as to why people were leaving, a primary reason was lack of career-development opportunities. Shawn realized the leaders in his organization were not skilled in intentional and ongoing development of the people on their teams. They were basically just meeting annually or once every two years for performance reviews, and the topic of career development was often not discussed. In the engagement surveys I have conducted with hundreds of organizations, lack of interest from employees' leaders around their career development was consistently at the top of their lists for leaving.

Shawn shared that coaching was a mystery to him, and he recognized the need to gain some skills himself. One of the greatest misconceptions about coaching is that it is all about teaching, but it's also about asking. Being able to ask the right questions is a key tool for coaching that promotes a dynamic two-way relationship with the person you are coaching and makes them an engaged and active part of the process. Asking questions also helps you to uncover current competencies, beliefs, challenges, and desires, just to name a few. This data allows you to focus your guidance and support on the person's individual needs. Asking good questions encourages critical thinking as you focus less on providing the right answer and more on helping the person navigate decision-making so they can grow competent and confident in their abilities.

I helped Shawn craft questions around the various topics that I have found to be essential regardless of the industry. We discovered that one reason people felt they weren't getting support in career development was because they were never asked about it! Over the next couple months, Shawn scheduled a series of one-on-ones with his key leaders to practice asking good questions and witnessing how that info naturally informed the best path for overall development. He received great feedback and additional input that we compiled to create that course for the leadership development program. Asking questions and genuinely listening has become a lost art. When leaders are intentional in these areas, a total transformation takes place that influences the most important components of the organization: engagement, performance, and retention.

The program launched with great success, and a recent engagement survey showed an increase, specifically citing Shawn and the leadership team's interest in their growth and career development.

ACTION STEP

Want to get results like Shawn's? Here's what you can do.

Create a Coaching Session Plan

1. Choose a specific person to coach. People generally need coaching for one of three reasons: (1) to improve performance, (2) to learn a new role, or (3) to guide their career path/promotion potential. If you have several people who need coaching, choose the one who you could impact the most.

2. Choose the areas of focus for coaching with the person you've selected.

- Technical (doing the job well)
- Interpersonal (working effectively with the team and clients)
- Leadership (creating engagement, performance, and retention)
- Business development (developing a client network and bringing in work)
- Career development (planning for growth and promotion)
- Work/life integration (managing time and stress levels)
- Other (any industry-specific areas of focus)

3. Plan your coaching session using the four Ds of appreciative inquiry, a series of four clarifying questions. They will provide structure for your sessions and give you plenty to talk about and follow up on. I have modified the questions for the coaching conversation. You can use these as is or

tweak them to fit your situation. Concentrate on the area of focus you selected in step #2.

1. Discovery: Where are you currently strong in this area?
2. Dream: If you were operating at your full potential in this area, what would that look like?
3. Design: What ideas do you have for how to reach your full potential?
4. Delivery: What actions would you like to take between now and the next time we meet?

4. Last, decide on how many coaching sessions you will have and schedule a regular cadence for sessions. Once or twice a month is typically helpful, and this cadence can be modified as needed. You can use the four Ds each time you meet to discuss progress and follow up on goals.

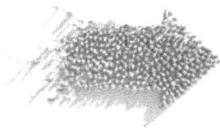

Day 25
The Power of Quiet Strength

Everyone shines, given the right lighting.

— SUSAN CAIN

One of the things I am most passionate about in my work is seeing diverse leaders get promoted and lead effectively in their own unique ways. My experience has taught me that there isn't one leadership prototype that is best. All types have both strengths and weaknesses. One thing I have often observed is introverted personality types getting overlooked in favor of more extroverted personality types. Not only does this limit the leadership pool within organizations, but it discourages introverts from seeing themselves as leaders. This could be because extroverts have more visible and obvious strengths while the strengths of introverts are less obvious. Introverted leaders have a quieter strength and offer much to their roles, such as great listening skills, taking time to think things through before making decisions, and remaining calm in stressful situations. On the flip side, a common struggle for introverted leaders is cultivating the more relational sides of the role. Whatever your personality type, this chapter is devoted to building that relational skill set.

Today, we're again working on increasing our levels of **interpersonal effectiveness**.

WHAT IS INTERPERSONAL EFFECTIVENESS?

We covered this skill on day 19, but it bears repeating: interpersonal effectiveness is the ability to make meaningful connections with others, regardless of our personality types or how they may differ from others. In the context of emotional intelligence at work, it means being intentional about considering the needs of others and adjusting our approaches to achieve shared goals.

BENEFITS OF INTERPERSONAL EFFECTIVENESS

Leaders strong in this skill are approachable, creating a safe space for their teams to ask questions and bring up concerns. They also make themselves accessible, communicating that they are available and care for their teams. They make it clear that team members can get their questions answered and can get the support they need to do good work. When leaders take an active interest in the needs of their team members, even when those needs are very different from their own, they communicate a sense of value and respect that is reciprocated by those they lead. Relationships between leaders and their teams change from purely transactional relationships focused on getting work done to transformational relationships where there is a sense of shared vision that people are inspired to go above and beyond to accomplish.

SYMPTOMS THAT YOU MAY NEED TO BUILD YOUR SKILL SET IN INTERPERSONAL EFFECTIVENESS

Introverts

- You avoid small talk and prefer to focus on the task at hand.
- You view social interactions as an inefficient use of time.
- You mostly enjoy working independently and have your door closed most of the time.

Extroverts

- You tend to jump in with opinions and solutions without getting feedback from others.
- You often talk more than you listen.
- You sometimes make rash decisions without thinking things through.

JEFF, CFO, GOVERNMENT AGENCY

Jeff is a master with numbers but felt a bit clumsy when it came to leading his team. When leaders go from individual contributors to leading a team, some never make the leap to truly embrace their new roles. What do I mean by this? As an individual contributor, you are focused on your own contributions and performance. As a leader, managing the performance of others (in addition to your job) becomes a primary function by which success and your value to the organization are measured. Some "leaders" never really become leaders except in title because they continue to operate independently and expect their teams to do the same. This is where Jeff was when I met him.

As his firm grew, Jeff was tasked with leading a team to meet the needs of an ever-growing client base. He reached out to me for coaching because he wondered how an introverted person could lead a team of social butterflies. As I mentioned before, I have experienced many different types of people becoming effective leaders when they are committed and determined to do so.

The recent feedback Jeff had received from his team during reviews was that he often came off as unfriendly and inaccessible (always having his door closed). Meetings were short and sweet and focused on task accomplishment. Individual members of the team didn't feel like they knew Jeff, making it easy to feel intimidated and reluctant to ask questions for fear of bothering him.

Jeff didn't deny the feedback and admitted that the social needs of his team felt overwhelming to him and like a distraction from getting work done. When people operate differently than you do, it's easy to focus on the frustrations about those differences rather than on the value that they bring. I asked Jeff to share with me why he thought the company hired social butterflies to work with him; he shared that those employees' roles were client-facing and they were excellent with clients. Next, I asked him to identify a reward (if any) of improving his interpersonal effectiveness with his team. He was a little stumped, so I suggested that if he gave his team what they needed, they would likely be motivated to work hard for him and give him what he needed.

Over the next couple of weeks, I suggested Jeff make some small tweaks that would make a big difference:

1. Smile more! Introverts are very internal, so they

have to be intentional about providing cues to others.

2. Allow for five minutes of small talk at the beginning of each meeting to show interest in others and share info about himself to help them to get to know him.

3. Schedule regular one-on-ones with team members to get to know them and ensure they have what they need to do their jobs.

4. Let his team know what his needs were.

In Jeff's case, he needed uninterrupted time every day to get work done, a task management system created to see the status of tasks and projects, and an understanding that meetings could be relational but also efficient. A key point to make here is that I don't believe a leader needs to change their core temperament, but I do believe they must be willing to meet their team's needs. In doing so, the leader almost always gets their needs met too when they make them known.

In just three short months, Jeff and his team created a great rhythm of working together where everyone's needs were known and met. His team shared how much they respected and appreciated Jeff's willingness to customize his leadership for them, motivating them to give him their best work. Jeff told me that he actually enjoyed leading now, something he had never thought he'd say!

ACTION STEP

Want to get results like Jeff's? Here's what you can do.

Complete the Team Needs and Actions Exercise

Get feedback from your team about their needs:

- What am I doing well that you would like me to continue doing as a leader?
- What are some things I could do more of or differently?

Based on the feedback you get, create a document with two columns, (1) team needs and (2) actions to take. Use the document to track your progress and note your team's performance and engagement as you do.

Day 26
The Power of the Ps

Communication is not about saying what we think. Communication is about ensuring others hear what we mean.

— SIMON SINEK

When I was in college, I changed my major ten times! Eventually, I ended up getting an undergrad degree in communications. I have some natural aptitude, but I was also drawn to the art of it. It's fascinating to me that two people can get a completely different outcome based on the quality of their communication.

The majority of my education was focused on speaking and writing, but I took a few electives in interpersonal and gender communication. These skills helped to set me apart and let me find success in a variety of industries that I never would have anticipated. I learned that communication is a tool for influence that can be incredibly empowering for leaders. In my consulting practice, I have found that often, leaders, teams, and organizations rise and fall on the quality of their communication. Communication is also the topic I am most often requested to focus on for trainings, coaching, and consulting. Companies are learning that an investment in better communication skills yields a multiplied return in many different areas. Whether it's in your professional or personal life, communication is often the golden thread that defines the quality of your relationships and the results you can achieve.

Today, we are focusing on increasing our skills in **communication**.

WHAT IS COMMUNICATION?

Communication is the ability to send and receive clear messages and be understood when doing so. In the context of emotional intelligence at work, cultivating communication means being intentional about our body language, tone, and choice of words to convey an effective message to different types of people. Leaders strong in this skill are great listeners and can adjust and customize their messages to make connections and influence others. They are clear, authentic, and positive. They know when to talk and when to listen. In my experience, skilled communication is one of the top three most important qualities for leaders to possess.

BENEFITS OF COMMUNICATION

When communication around tasks and expectations is clear, leaders have more productive teams. Teams are also more engaged with communication in the form of feedback, as it provides people with the information they need to succeed in their work and roles. When leaders customize their message to individuals and groups, there is greater buy-in for decisions and more commitment to seeing them through. Leaders who communicate proactively during change or conflict create a sense of trust and loyalty within their teams.

SYMPTOMS THAT YOU MAY NEED TO BUILD YOUR SKILL SET IN COMMUNICATION

- You tend to communicate off the cuff without much forethought.
- You notice that your intended message is not always what is received by others.
- You find it challenging to get people on board with your ideas.

JOHN, CREATIVE DIRECTOR, MARKETING AND BRANDING AGENCY

John is an intelligent creative. When he reached out for coaching, he was seeking to improve his communication skills. When he presented his ideas to others, he noticed that people didn't pay attention to him and tuned him out. He had received consistent feedback that he was often overly detailed and wordy. People wanted the big-picture, high-level vision for proposed campaigns without getting lost in the weeds.

John didn't understand why knowing details wasn't important to key decision-makers. I shared with John the importance of customizing your communication to your audience rather than just defaulting to your natural communication style. One of the most popular trainings I deliver with organizations is called Core Strengths; this training provides tools for evaluating the motives of others and adjusting your communication accordingly. There are three primary motives: people, performance, and process.

In a nutshell, those who have a people orientation are interested in how their words and actions will impact people and prefer communication that is relational and tells a story. Those with a performance orientation are driven to get things done and want bulleted big-picture communication focused on results. Those with a process orientation want to get things right and prefer communication with lots of details.

The first thing I prompted John to do was to identify the motives of the key decision-makers he was presenting to. He speculated that they were performance driven. With that in mind, I suggested that he customize his communication at the next meeting by providing a high-level overview of the project that touched on the major components of the project and what results would be achieved. He could then open the floor for questions and provide more detail as people requested it. Those with a performance motive, like the decision-makers John would be speaking with, generally prefer communication that is short and sweet.

When John changed how he communicated, the response he got was drastically different! People were engaged, asked questions, and noted how clear the information was. John was amazed at how quickly things shifted with the right tools after years of ineffective meetings.

We continued to build John's skill set in customizing his communication according to the motives of his audience. Eventually, he was able to find great success in client meetings and presentations as well! As a leader, one of your greatest superpowers of influence lies in your ability to communicate effectively with lots of different types of people. Communication is a worthy investment with a guaranteed return!

ACTION STEP

Want to get results like John's? Here's what you can do.

Communication Game Plan

Choose a person you would like to communicate with more effectively. This could be someone in your organization or team, or it could be a client. Assess which of the three core motives applies to that person: people, performance, or process.

Based on the person's motives, plan your next interaction with them.

- **People:** Make a personal connection before discussing work, show appreciation for something specific they've done, and connect your proposed ideas with their benefit to people.
- **Performance:** Get straight to the point, keep your communication brief, and include impact and results.
- **Process:** Skip the small talk and focus on the structure and details of the task at hand, describe any facts to support a particular direction, and give them time to think it over.

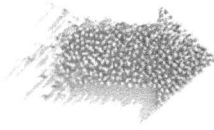

Day 27
It's Not You, It's Me

I love mankind...it's people I can't stand!!

— CHARLES M. SCHULZ

The ability to navigate conflict effectively is a skill set I wish was taught in school. In general, people learn these skills because they either observed someone who modeled them well or made intentional efforts to learn them through a course, reading, coaching, or otherwise. The ability to address conflict productively can make or break relationships. A lack of skill can cause irreversible damage, whereas having strong skills can deepen the trust and intimacy in a relationship. While it's important to develop a skill set to navigate conflict in your own situations, as a leader, you will also be called upon to help facilitate good conflict resolution between members of your team. The skills you will learn in today's reading will offer principles to address both.

Today, we are focusing on increasing our skills in **conflict management**.

WHAT IS CONFLICT MANAGEMENT?

Conflict management is the ability to effectively address and resolve disagreements. In the context of emotional intelligence at work, cultivating skills in conflict management means communicating assertively but respectfully, listening to and collaborating with others, and seeing the process through until it's resolved. Leaders strong in this skill move toward conflict and are able to de-escalate tense situations. They are able to draw out others, consider others' perspectives, and create win-wins. In my experience, skills in effective conflict resolution are some of the most important yet most undertrained competencies in leaders. Typically, I find that leaders fall at two extreme ends of a continuum: either they address conflict directly but ineffectively, or they avoid conflict and problems go unaddressed.

BENEFITS OF CONFLICT MANAGEMENT

Leaders who are strong in this skill are not only able to navigate their own conflicts but are also good at helping their team members resolve conflicts with one another. As a result, they create cultures that move toward conflict rather than avoid it. When conflicts are managed well and resolved, people are able to trust one another, stay aligned, and work collaboratively to get things done. There is a decrease in stress and in the number of sick days people take. Good talent is retained, and the time and resources required to rehire and train people is reduced. While it may be seemingly hard to quantify, unresolved conflict does have a tangible cost.

SYMPTOMS THAT YOU MAY NEED TO BUILD YOUR SKILL SET IN CONFLICT MANAGEMENT

- You tend to avoid conflict rather than moving toward it.
- If you do address conflict, the situation seems to get worse instead of getting resolved.
- You have trouble helping others on your team resolve their conflicts.

JAKE AND DEBORAH, SENIOR LEADERS, CITY PLANNING

Jake and Deborah had worked together for the city for many years, and they had fought from day one! The city manager finally reached out to me to request some mediation work with them. She valued them each individually, as they were very good at their jobs, but wherever there was crossover in their roles, a huge conflict would result. The city manager didn't want to have to fire anybody, but she also didn't know how much longer she could tolerate the dysfunction; their relationship was affecting the morale of the entire office.

There are a couple key principles surrounding conflict that I want to highlight here. Regardless of the conflict, these factors are often at play. The first principle is the importance of getting everyone in the room together. When I met with Jake and Deborah individually, they shared completely different perspectives about the same events, whereas when we all met together, they were more measured with their words and accountable for how they portrayed one another's actions. When Jake and Deborah heard one another's perspectives for the first time, each realized that they had made inaccurate assumptions about the other's actions. They had failed to ask what the other meant or what they intended in their interactions. Typically, when there is ongoing conflict, getting everyone in the same room can bring the necessary clarity to move the conversation forward productively.

A second principle at play is safety. If there is not a sense of safety in the relationship, people are not going to address the conflict. A safe conversation is one where different ideas and perspectives can be discussed without the fear of things getting personal. Some examples of things getting personal are name-calling, belittling or dismissive comments, and threats or negative repercussions for bringing things up. Despite working closely together, Jake and Deborah could not have a conflict without it getting personal and demoralizing. When this happens, new ground rules for working together have to be established to create safety. I helped Jake and Deborah create their own ground rules. Some of the things they came up with were listening to one another without interruption, asking for clarification when triggered instead of just reacting, and managing emotions in such a way that it reestablished a sense of safety. I was there to be the gatekeeper at first, but eventually, the two were able to self-regulate and be gatekeepers with one another in a respectful way.

A third principle present in most conflicts is a moment of broken trust. Once trust is broken, it is very hard to regain it. If trust can be regained by putting the two principles already described in place (talking directly to one another and in a safe environment), then the right environment has now been created to uncover and discuss when trust was broken. I facilitated a conversation between Jake and Deborah where they were able to identify the exact incident where trust had initially been broken. They both realized after hearing one another out that the incident had been a big misunderstanding. In other cases, it is necessary for both parties to take accountability before they can move forward.

Once the initial incident of broken trust was repaired, we had some legs to stand on to create a new relationship for the future. I encouraged Jake and Deborah to come up with some agreements to protect their relationship going forward. In addition to the other things already mentioned, they committed to going directly to one another with any issues instead of talking with others in the office about them.

By addressing the three principles present in nearly every conflict, Jake and Deborah were able to transform their working relationship from one they merely tolerated into one they enjoyed. The whole office benefited when Jake and Deborah learned the skills of conflict management. Ultimately, the impact was twofold—a more peaceful office and leaders modeling how to navigate conflict well.

Whether you are involved in your own conflict or are helping others navigate theirs, the above three principles are a helpful framework for creating structure around an often messy process.

ACTION STEP

Want to get results like Jake and Deborah's? Here's what you can do.

Learning from Past Conflict

Choose a past conflict and reflect on the three principles discussed.

The first principle is the importance of getting everyone in the room together.

CHAPTER 27

Questions:

- Was everyone who was involved in the conflict brought together to work through the conflict?
- Did each person have the opportunity to share their perspective?
- Were assumptions about the other party's actions or words clarified or cleared up?

The second principle is safety.

Questions:

- Were people respectful to one another (ex. no name-calling, belittling or dismissive comments, or threats or negative repercussions for bringing things up)?
- Were different ideas discussed without personal attacks?
- Did people listen to one another without interruption, ask for clarification when triggered instead of reacting, and manage their emotions well?

The third principle is a moment of broken trust.

Questions:

- Was the initial incident that caused the conflict discussed?
- Was there clarity that highlighted a misunderstanding?
- Were people accountable if they needed to own their parts?

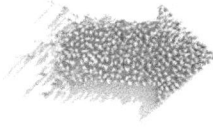

Day 28
The Importance of
Fingerprints

If people don't weigh in, they can't buy in.

— PATRICK LENCIONI

One of the marks of memorable leaders is their ability to inspire others to act and contribute to a vision and purpose larger than themselves. Inspirational leaders are able to capture the heart to mobilize people to do extraordinary things. When I think of inspirational leaders, I think of Martin Luther King Jr. when he delivered his "I Have a Dream" speech. Despite the racial challenges of the day, King invited people to rise above the current reality toward a promising vision of a better future. Other inspiring leaders include Mahatma Gandhi, Winston Churchill, Albert Einstein, Abraham Lincoln, and Nelson Mandela, as they all shared strong characteristics: clear conviction and purpose, vision, and the ability to inspire others to action around their causes.

Many leaders I've worked with believe they don't have the

natural charisma to be inspirational. But my experience has taught me that leaders can grow in any area they commit themselves to.

Today, we are focusing on increasing our levels of **inspirational leadership**.

WHAT IS INSPIRATIONAL LEADERSHIP?

Inspirational leadership is a style of leadership that captures not just the heads but also the hearts of those one leads. The word *inspire* means "to excite, encourage, or breathe life into."[1] In the context of cultivating emotional intelligence at work, it means bringing out the best in people to accomplish big things together. Leaders strong in this skill articulate a clear and compelling vision for the future. They also create a sense of common purpose beyond the day-to-day tasks that motivate and compel others toward action. They are good at big-picture thinking and not getting stuck in the weeds of the everyday.

In my experience, having a clear vision and communicating it often is one of the top three skills of a standout leader. It can also be one of the most challenging, as some leaders struggle to find clarity.

BENEFITS OF INSPIRATIONAL LEADERSHIP

One of the main benefits of inspirational leadership is that it compels people to be not just compliant in their work, but truly committed. Leaders strong in this skill offer a compelling invitation to be a part of something bigger than themselves, tied to a strong sense of purpose. This creates an

---

1. Vocabulary.com, "inspire," accessed January 6, 2024, https://www.vocabulary.com/dictionary/inspire.

enthusiasm for doing work that feels important and meaningful. There is a sense of belonging and alignment as people's passions are ignited to create a desired future together. Leaders who inspire create unstoppable teams who move beyond the status quo to achieve extraordinary things.

SYMPTOMS THAT YOU MAY NEED TO BUILD YOUR SKILL SET IN INSPIRATIONAL LEADERSHIP

- You don't have a clear vision for the future.
- You tend to focus your efforts on the tasks at hand instead of thinking about the big picture.
- You notice that your team is more compliant than committed.

HELEN, PRESIDENT, NONPROFIT

When I met Helen, she was nearing the end of her career, but she still had a desire to spend her remaining years before retirement doing meaningful work. She had spent her career in a variety of high-profile leadership roles and wanted to give back by serving as president of one of her favorite nonprofits.

Despite her success, there was one piece of constructive feedback that she had taken to heart and wanted to focus on developing in her new role. She was consistently described as intelligent, thorough, and task driven but lacking the qualities of an inspirational leader. She desired to be this kind of leader, especially for an organization with a cause close to her heart, but she didn't know where to start. She wondered if being an inspirational leader was a personality trait or something that could be learned.

From my experience working with thousands of leaders of

all personality types, I have learned that becoming an inspirational leader is absolutely possible for anyone! All of the skills in this book can be learned with practice if you are willing and committed. Inspiring others toward action attached to purpose will create a team that isn't just compliant to complete tasks but truly committed to the mission and vision of the organization as a whole.

Since Helen was a leader new to the organization, I suggested that she get a sense of where the organization had been and what some of her team's desires and dreams were for the future. Many leaders make the mistake of creating a vision themselves and announcing it to everyone. This creates very little commitment and buy-in; the secret is to create a sense of shared vision.

The four Ds of appreciative inquiry (which we discussed on day 24) are an amazing tool for facilitating feedback and generating ideas with your team. I helped Helen prepare for her first meeting with her team by covering the first two Ds, discovery (in this case, I asked, "What has the organization done well that you think should continue?") and dream (for which I asked, "If the organization were to more fully realize its potential this year, describe what that would look like."). These first two Ds are the vision piece of the four Ds. During her meeting, Helen captured the common themes for both questions, which helped the team focus on building on their current strengths and get excited about the future. She captured the themes of the team's responses and added some additional thoughts about her future aspirations for the organization. She crafted the themes into a clear and compelling vision statement that everybody saw their fingerprints on.

In the months that followed, Helen covered the final two Ds: design (for which she asked her team, "What ideas do you have for accomplishing the vision [dream] we created together?") and delivery (for which she asked, "What contribution or area would you like to own to help realize the vision?"). Helen had the vision printed and hung in a central location where it could be revisited often. She also created a document that listed the ideas and roles for each person on the team. Helen felt different, leading this team from the start. She described herself as leading from the heart, an experience that was new to her and at the core of inspirational leadership.

In the years that followed, Helen continued to communicate the vision behind the everyday tasks with her team with much success. She is now described as a leader who took the organization to new heights because of her inspirational leadership!

ACTION STEP

Want to get results like Helen's? Here's what you can do.

Create a Vision Statement

Start with the first two Ds by asking the following:

1. **Discovery:** What has the organization done well that you think should continue?
2. **Dream:** If the organization were to more fully realize its potential this year, describe what that would look like.

Capture the themes and then create a short vision statement. Here are some examples to draw from:

- Coca-Cola: "Refresh the world and make a

difference."[2]

- JFK: "To put a man on the moon by the end of the decade."[3]
- Amazon: "[To be] Earth's most customer-centric company, best employer, and safest place to work."[4]

Once you have a clear and compelling vision statement, place it in a central location and refer to it often.

2. "Purpose & Vision," The Coca-Cola Company, accessed January 7, 2025, https://www.coca-colacompany.com/about-us/purpose-and-vision.

3. "This Week in NASA History: JFK's Moon Challenge," APPEL Knowledge Services, NASA, February 28, 2010, https://appel.nasa.gov/2010/02/28/ao_2-3_sf_history-html/.

4. "Amazon Leadership Principles," Amazon, accessed January 7, 2025, https://www.aboutamazon.com/about-us/leadership-principles.

Conclusion

Congrats! If you are reading this, you have made it to the end of twenty-eight days of building some of the most important skills for transforming your leadership. If you took the daily actions, you should've had some significant shifts in your leadership confidence, seen a difference in how your team responds to you (particularly in the areas of engagement, retention, and performance), and experienced more enjoyment in leading.

So what's next? Since these are skills that will continue to be developed over the lifetime of your leadership, I recommend going back through the book and revisiting the chapters that are most applicable to your current circumstances or challenges with your team.

Remember, just reading the chapters without doing the suggested action steps will not change anything. It would be like reading a recipe and never actually cooking the dish. You get proficient by getting reps around each skill.

As you are building your skill set, I strongly encourage you to include your team! My online course Leading with

Emotional Intelligence is a great option for growing in these skills together. You will get access to on-demand videos and a downloadable workbook with exercises and actions you can put into practice right away. For an even more interactive experience, there's an option to meet virtually each month with one of our certified coaches, who will show you how to apply these new skills to your real-time leadership challenges. For more information, go to my website: www.elise boggs.com/courses.

Want to go even deeper? Subscribe to my podcast, *12min-leadership*, where in 12 minutes or less I'll share small things that you can put into immediate practice that will make a big difference in your leadership effectiveness.

If you need more hands-on support, work with us! Our team boasts decades of combined executive-level leadership experience in a variety of industries offering consulting, training, and coaching services. Whatever the challenge or goal, we can help you create a customized strategy to help you achieve your goals quickly! Go to my website for more information: www.eliseboggs.com.

Creating your dream team is not wishful thinking; it is the product of a focus on the right skills that build a sense of connection and strong relationships with your team. For the past seventeen years, I have watched many frustrated leaders overcome seemingly impossible challenges with their teams by applying the skills in this book. I invite you to become one of those leaders. While at times it may seem easier to go alone, you'll go farther together, and if you do, you'll enjoy the ride a lot more!

About the Author

Elise is a certified emotional intelligence coach, a leadership coach and consultant, and a TEDx speaker. She holds a master's degree in organizational leadership and development. Since 2008, she has supported the development of thousands of leaders across many different industries including the military (working with the US Navy SEALs), medicine, law enforcement, engineering, architecture, wealth management, and city leadership and has helped them get incredible results *through* their teams.

Her career began in the nonprofit sector, where she oversaw a large unpaid staff of volunteers. This became a lab for learning what drives people to engage and perform at high levels. She tested out different leadership approaches, and when the volunteers began to outperform the paid staff, she knew she was on to something!

Since then, she's made it her mission to help bridge the

gap in knowledge for intelligent, competent, high-achieving leaders—leaders who are feeling stuck and frustrated because they are not getting the results they know they are capable of from their teams. No matter your industry, becoming a skilled leader will profoundly impact the team you are able to create and the results you can achieve.

Elise is the founder of Elise Boggs Consulting, a boutique consulting firm specializing in creating high performance leaders and teams. She resides in sunny San Diego with her husband, daughter, and golden retriever.

www.ingramcontent.com/pod-product-compliance
Lightning Source LLC
Chambersburg PA
CBHW071604210326
41597CB00019B/3393